VERA WANG

ASIAN AMERICANS OF ACHIEVEMENT

Margaret Cho

Daniel Inouye

Michelle Kwan

Bruce Lee

Maya Lin

Yo-Yo Ma

Isamu Noguchi

Amy Tan

Vera Wang

Kristi Yamaguchi

ASIAN AMERICANS
OF ACHIEVEMENT

VERA WANG

ANNE M. TODD

CHELSEA HOUSE
PUBLISHERS
An imprint of Infobase Publishing

Vera Wang

Copyright © 2007 by Infobase Publishing

All rights reserved. No part of this book may be reproduced or utilized in
any form or by any means, electronic or mechanical, including photocopying,
recording, or by any information storage or retrieval systems, without
permission in writing from the publisher. For information contact:

Chelsea House
An imprint of Infobase Publishing
132 West 31st Street
New York, NY 10001

ISBN-10: 0-7910-9272-0
ISBN-13: 978-0-7910-9272-9

Library of Congress Cataloging-in-Publication Data
Todd, Anne M.
  Vera Wang / Anne M. Todd.
    p. cm.
  Includes bibliographical references and index.
  ISBN 0-7910-9272-0 (hardcover)
  1. Wang, Vera. 2. Women fashion designers—New York (State)—New York—
Biography. I. Title.
  TT505.W36T63 2007
  746.9'2092—dc22
  [B]   2006028386

Chelsea House books are available at special discounts when purchased in
bulk quantities for businesses, associations, institutions, or sales promotions.
Please call our Special Sales Department in New York at (212) 967-8800
or (800) 322-8755.

You can find Chelsea House on the World Wide Web at
http://www.chelseahouse.com

Series design by Erika K. Arroyo
Cover design by Ben Peterson

Printed in the United States of America

Bang EJB 10 9 8 7 6 5 4 3 2 1

This book is printed on acid-free paper.

All links and Web addresses were checked and verified to be correct at the time of
publication. Because of the dynamic nature of the Web, some addresses and links
may have changed since publication and may no longer be valid.

CONTENTS

Style on Ice

When figure skater Nancy Kerrigan took the ice in the 1994 Winter Olympics in Lillehammer, Norway, the world stopped to stare. Kerrigan's simple, champagne-colored skating dress was far different from the typical flashy designs of the 1990s. Most skating outfits of the time were brightly colored and gaudy, with sparkling sequins and revealing necklines. Kerrigan's tastefully muted, sophisticated skating outfit boasted 11,500 tiny hand-sewn beads and illusion sleeves, at a cost of $13,000.

The designer behind the unique dress was Vera Wang, and this skating outfit alone soon made her a household name. The outfit embraced what Wang believes: Modern is unpredictable. Wang's designs took skating fashion in a new direction. Soon after the 1994 Olympics, Wang's career took off. Vera Wang had started in the fashion business designing wedding dresses and bridal-related dresses (bridesmaids', flower girls', and so on) nearly exclusively. After the Olympics, Wang broadened her design collection to include eveningwear and daywear.

U.S. figure skater Nancy Kerrigan, wearing a costume designed by Vera Wang, gives a silver medal performance in the women's free skating program at Hamar Olympic Amphitheatre in Norway in 1994.

Fashion designer Vera Wang arrives at the 2003 Council of Fashion Design Awards wearing one of her creations.

You will most often find Vera Wang—a lean and fit Chinese-American woman with long, straight, jet-black hair—in black leggings and something layered on top, perhaps misbuttoned, usually very expensive, and always with a purpose. Vera Wang lives and breathes clothes. She constantly seeks new ways to design clothes with edge and style. When she was a young girl shopping with her fashionable mother in New York City and Paris, Wang developed a passion for clothes: Every zipper, every tuck, every seam had a purpose, and she loved to think about how to make clothing that would allow the woman wearing it to shine through and feel great about herself.

In addition to designing for Nancy Kerrigan, Wang has designed for other elite figure skaters, including Peggy Fleming and Michelle Kwan. Wang finds designing skating costumes challenging because of the need to find fabrics that flex and recover with the extreme twists and bends of a figure skater's movements; it is a challenge that she relishes.

The successes of the skating outfits, which brought Wang international fame and recognition, have a sentimental pleasure for her, as well. Wang had grown up as a competitive figure skater, so designing skating costumes joined two of her great loves. Wang understands firsthand the rotations that a skater's body makes and how the costume must move with the skater. Wang had Olympic dreams of her own, so she knew that an Olympic skating costume must suit not only the skater, but also the country she represents when standing on the podium. Wang considered all of these aspects as she sat down to design the 1994 Olympic skating costume for Nancy Kerrigan. Although Wang never made it to the Olympics as a skater, her designs and her sense of style did.

2

Beginnings

Vera Ellen Wang was born on June 27, 1949, in New York City. Her parents, Cheng Ching and Florence Wang, were both born in China. The couple married in 1939 and then fled China in 1947 after the Communist takeover. They arrived in New York with dreams of freedom and self-expression. They would share those dreams with their two American-born children, Vera and Kenneth.

Cheng Ching and Florence had lived a life of prestige and wealth in China. They maintained that refined lifestyle on the Upper East Side of Manhattan, in New York. They preserved their connection to China through Asian food and customs; Cheng Ching also started a business in Singapore. In New York, they visited art museums, dined at fine restaurants, and enjoyed the theater. The Wangs passed their sophisticated sense of style and fashion, their appreciation of the arts, and their love of fine things to their children, who had a comfortable childhood with a great many opportunities offered to them.

FLORENCE WU

Florence Wu was born in 1918 as the youngest daughter of General Wu Jing Biao and Wu Yue Shin. Because her mother was the daughter of a feudal Chinese warlord, Florence grew up in palaces and summer mansions. Most young girls in China were not encouraged to get an education, and even fewer were encouraged to pursue higher education at universities. Florence was an exception: She received a bachelor of arts degree from Xi Nan University. After relocating to New York City, she became a translator for the United Nations.

In addition to her work, Florence had a passion for beautiful things. She took young Vera with her when she traveled to Paris to shop for new clothes. Vera later referred to her mother as "the old-fashioned definition of a clotheshorse, much like a Babe Paley or a Jackie O." Florence loved clothes, and her tall, slender frame was easy and fun to dress. Florence shopped for clothes around the world, and her artistic nature allowed her to see "outside the box," ignoring mainstream trends. She intentionally used her clothes as an expression of who she was. Vera later described her mother as "ahead of her time" in terms of wearing unusual fashions before they were "in." Florence encouraged Vera to seek an art that would allow her to express herself as well. Like her mother, Vera found the world of fashion intriguing and fulfilling.

CHENG CHING WANG

Cheng Ching Wang grew up in Shanghai, China. His father was a war minister under Chiang Kai-shek, a Chinese Nationalist leader. Cheng Ching began his education in China but came to the United States to finish his graduate work at the Massachusetts Institute of Technology (MIT). He moved to Singapore temporarily while he started an oil company called the Oceanic Petroleum Corporation, which he still oversees today.

Like his wife did, Cheng Ching has an eye for fashionable clothing and dresses himself impeccably. His attention to fashion ends there, however. Foremost, Cheng Ching is a business-person who appreciates the bottom line. In addition to his oil company, Cheng Ching is the president and chairperson of the U.S. Summit Corporation, an international trading company that deals primarily with food and pharmaceuticals.

FROM NEW YORK TO PARIS

The Wangs spent most school months in New York City and summers in Paris. Growing up, Vera saw firsthand when the Beatles made it big in Europe, watched now-famous designer Betsey Johnson make a name for herself in New York, saw model Brigitte Bardot make waves on beaches of France, and took in all the sights and culture that these two cities had to offer. Florence and Cheng Ching felt strongly about the importance of the arts and education: They made a point of exposing their children to museums and fashion in Europe and New York in hopes of broadening their minds and spirits.

Sometimes, Florence and Vera would go to Paris for shopping and fashion shows to get some quality time together. Instead of flying, they would travel by boat, the *Queen Mary.* Wang later said in an article in *Travel and Leisure,* "What a fantasyland—I had free run of the ship. Back then, travel wasn't about speed, it was about the process."

Once in Paris, they roomed at fancy hotels, such as Plaza Athénée. They frequently attended *haute couture* (a French phrase that literally means "high sewing") shows in Paris to view the very latest in fashion and trends. Christian Dior, Givenchy, and Balenciaga were a few of the shows that the mother-daughter team viewed regularly. Throughout her childhood, Vera was exposed to both dramatic and subtle changes in fashion trends and styles. She knew the names of all of the fashion designers and watched as fashions evolved—for better or worse.

Wang attended many fashion shows in Paris with her mother. It is likely she was later inspired by Christian Dior's simple white wedding gown from his 1968 collection, shown here.

OLYMPIC DREAMS

Vera Wang had a busy childhood; her parents believed in an active lifestyle. As a result, Wang took figure skating, ballet, piano, and tennis lessons. She has continued her active lifestyle as an adult, adding golf to her list of enjoyed sports.

At seven, Wang received her first pair of figure skates. She fell in love with skating. Her father also knew how to figure skate: He had picked up the sport during his youth in China. By the age of 10, Vera began to win championships as a figure skater. Sonya Dunfield, Vera's coach, taught her at the Skating Club of New York. Vera was dedicated and serious about skating. She practiced long hours and gave the sport her full attention while practicing. Spectators delighted in her talent and artistry on the ice. Early in her skating career, she set her sights on the Olympics. She dreamed of standing on the winners' podium one day.

Fellow skaters and coaches noted years later that it was not only on the ice where Vera was noticed—her sense of style and manner always stood out. In an interview in *20/20 Magazine* as an adult, Wang said, "I was always involved in all aspects of skating, not just the technique, the choreography, the music, but the visual aspects, too—how I looked, what I should wear."

Part of her time off the ice was spent creating sketches of skaters in various skating costumes—her first attempts at fashion design. Wang would sketch out costumes she hoped to wear when skating. At the time, her mind was set on becoming a professional skater, but with her sketches she was unintentionally laying the groundwork for the path she would eventually follow: fashion.

In addition to figure skating, Vera studied ballet at George Balanchine's School of American Ballet, located in New York City's Lincoln Center. The prestigious school is one of the best dance schools in the country. Between her hours on the ice and in the dance studio, Vera became familiar with how the human body moves and came to better understand grace and poise. With the long hours spent in front of a mirror while dancing, she became aware of shape and proportion and how the parts of a whole fit together. She could look at a sketch or photograph and easily envision it as three-dimensional. Throughout her career, Wang has striven to make all of those dimensions work smoothly to create something beautiful.

BIG CHANGES

School was always an important part of Vera Wang's young life. She loves to learn and make more of herself—two qualities she believes that she inherited from her parents' Chinese roots. Her parents also placed a high priority on their children's education, and they expected their children to work hard and prosper.

HAUTE COUTURE

Vera Wang attended many haute couture shows as a young girl with her mother in Paris. *Haute couture* is a French phrase that means "high sewing," or "high fashion." Haute couture can refer to either the fashions themselves or the designers who create them. The term refers to exclusive, one-of-a-kind, often trendsetting fashions that are entirely hand sewn. Haute couture designs are cut and hand-fit to conform to a specific individual's body, resulting in a made-to-order garment. For instance, as Vera Wang wrote in her book, *Vera Wang on Weddings,* haute couture wedding gowns "are entirely handmade and decorated . . . [they] require extensive labor, which is usually reflected in the price. Couture fashion houses do require a minimum of four fittings; there are very few haute couture clients in the world."

The largest haute couture houses today are Giorgio Armani, Chanel, Christian Dior, Christian Lacroix, Givenchy, Yves Saint Laurent, and Valentino. Catering to wealthy and elite socialites, haute couture houses use the most expensive, luxurious fabrics in the world, such as silk, wool, cashmere, linen, leather, suede, and fur. The garments that haute couture houses create often influence the direction of mainstream fashion trends and styles.

Vera attended a prestigious all-girls prep school called the Chapin School (founded by Maria Bowen Chapin), located in New York City. The school runs from kindergarten to twelfth grade, catering to Manhattan's elite. The rigorous workload demands both strong study skills and a respect for learning. Vera embodied both traits: She studied hard and took her education seriously.

During her years at Chapin, Vera had become one of figure skating's elite, and she had dreams of making the 1968 Olympic

Most designers who create the exclusive haute couture fashions also depend on ready-to-wear collections, or fashions produced in multiples in standard clothing sizes. The ready-to-wear collections are needed for economic balance, as they bring in a higher return on the original investment. Yves Saint Laurent is one such designer. He made a highly successful transition between haute couture and ready-to-wear.

Saint Laurent was born in Algeria and then went to Paris to train at the Chambre Syndicale de la Haute Couture. Saint Laurent started his fashion career as an assistant to Christian Dior. Saint Laurent took over as the company's haute couture designer after Dior's death in 1957. Saint Laurent opened his own shop in 1962 on the rue Spontini, where Vera Wang enjoyed shopping during her college days. Here, Saint Laurent began his own line with an Yves Saint Laurent label. When he introduced his ready-to-wear clothing, it instantly became highly sought-after. From Paris to New York, consumers clamored to get the latest fashions by Saint Laurent.

Vera Wang likewise began in haute couture fashion and, although it took a few years longer, has since expanded to include a flourishing ready-to-wear line. Wang will continue to create haute couture fashions for celebrities and socialites, but now she is working to bring her name to an even broader clientele.

Ice skating legend Peggy Fleming competed at the U.S. Figure Skating Championship in 1967, winning the free skate title that year. She and former competitor Vera Wang later became friends.

team in the pairs division. Vera left Chapin during her junior year in order to direct her full attention and concentration to the upcoming 1968 Olympic Games, but she did not do it for the glory. When she skated her best, Vera felt proud of her performance—regardless of how she was judged. It was for this personal feeling of accomplishment that she so loved the sport. Vera competed at the U.S. Figure Skating Championships, where she placed fifth with her skating partner, James Stuart. The couple failed to make the U.S. Olympic team and later failed to make the World team. Vera was devastated.

Soon after these failures, Stuart decided to abandon pairs skating and skate as a single. He hoped he would have a better chance at success that way. Vera found herself without a partner. She felt lost and uncertain of what to do next. Until now, her goal of making the Olympic team had been foremost in her mind. Although Vera did some exhibition skating after failing to make the Olympic team, it seemed that competitive figure skating was not a viable career. Vera was not interested in touring with an ice show or teaching or coaching beginners, which seemed to be the only skating options left. After long hours considering her choices, she decided to give up on professional skating at the age of 19. It would take a long time for her to recover from this disappointment.

COLLEGE DAYS

Until this time, Wang had had a goal and a clear direction for her life—making the Olympic team as a figure skater. When that dream ended, she needed to find a new life plan. Wang enrolled at Sarah Lawrence College, located in Bronxville, New York, as a drama and premed student. She soon switched her major to art history, something in which she had always had a great interest.

Wang spent one year abroad, attending the Sorbonne in Paris. The Sorbonne, part of the University of Paris, is among Europe's most important universities. Wang studied art history there, returning to the city she frequented as a young girl. While studying in Paris, Wang lived at her parents' Paris apartment, located on the rue Spontini and within walking distance of upscale boutique Yves Saint Laurent. Wang returned home to spend her summer in New York.

In 1970, Wang took on her first working experience during her summer home from school. She was a salesperson and then later a window dresser at New York's Yves Saint Laurent boutique, located on Madison Avenue. The store was the height of sophistication and cutting-edge fashion. The two-story boutique looked modern and sleek, with black tiled floors, marble columns, and mirrored walls. Wang enjoyed its ambience and working with such fine clothing and product.

During Wang's time at Yves Saint Laurent, she met Frances Patiky Stein, an editor with prestigious fashion magazine *Vogue*. Wang charmed Stein, and Stein saw talent and spark in Wang. Wang was dressed impeccably and had an apparent knowledge and keen understanding of fashion. Stein told Wang to call her when she had completed college—perhaps there would be a position open at *Vogue*.

Once Wang had her college degree in 1971, she thought about what she wanted to do next. What she really wanted was to go back to school and study fashion; she had her eye on the Fashion Institute of Technology in New York City. Her father was unwilling to pay for fashion school, however. Cheng Ching *was* willing to pay for law school or business school, but Vera wasn't interested. She decided to call Stein in the hope of getting what she wanted from the fashion institute through on-the-job training. Wang did land a job with *Vogue*: She would assist Baron Nicolas de Gunzburg, a senior fashion editor, as well as Elsa Klensch, a senior fashion editor, and Grace Mirabella, the editor in chief.

3

From *Vogue* to Ralph Lauren

When Vera Wang appeared for her first day of work at *Vogue*, she wore a fancy outfit from Yves Saint Laurent with her hair and nails perfectly done. When the editors saw her, they said, "Go home and get changed because you're going to be doing dirt work." Wang, who prefers comfortable clothes to dressing up, was all too happy to comply. This was exactly the part of fashion Wang loved most—the nitty-gritty, hands-on figuring-out-what-looks-best-on-the-model, and minimizing or maximizing as needed.

A MAGAZINE WITH A HISTORY

Vogue magazine began in 1892 as a weekly society paper. Then in 1909, Condé Nast, a young publisher, bought the paper and began to transform it into the successful magazine it is today. He switched the weekly publication to a bimonthly format. The magazine included cultural information as well as biographies and news about artists, musicians, writers, and designers, with the goal to inform and educate

Anna Wintour and Vera Wang became friends at *Vogue* magazine. Wintour, seen here attending Wang's 2005 show, is very supportive of Wang's work.

the public about fashion around the country and around the world. In 1913, the magazine started to include photography. Over the years, *Vogue* became a highly successful and respected women's fashion magazine.

From 1963 to June 1971, Diana Vreeland was editor in chief of *Vogue*. She brought an exciting, cutting-edge style to the magazine. She devoted more pages to fashion and brought in a vibrant energy with bright colors and a feeling of fun and playfulness. Vreeland frequently featured photographs of supermodel Twiggy (Leslie Hornsby), originally from England. Twiggy brought a fresh, young look to *Vogue*, urging women's fashions toward looking younger and more carefree.

From July 1971 to October 1988, Grace Mirabella acted as editor in chief. She was more sedate and less playful than Diana Vreeland; for example, she painted over Vreeland's red office walls with beige paint. Likewise, Mirabella's years at *Vogue* brought on a sense of repetition that reviewers later criticized. During Mirabella's days at *Vogue*, the magazine focused on women's changing lives. Photographs showed models wearing jeans and women both at the workplace and at home as well as at gala events. She also replaced some of the photography that had been introduced by Vreeland with articles about fitness, health, and food.

Anna Wintour is *Vogue*'s current editor in chief; she has held the position since November 1988. She turned the magazine around by bringing in a fresh look and feel. Wintour is a powerful—sometimes feared—master of fashion, and she immediately brought fashion back to center stage in *Vogue*.

Today, Wintour and Wang are close friends. Wang's brother, Kenneth, at one time dated Wintour. At *Vogue*, Wintour is working to reach a broader audience by including tips to readers on how to achieve runway looks without spending a great deal of money. She is also striving to get the fashions of new designers photographed and known through exposure in the magazine.

PROJECT RUNWAY

The fashion industry is highly competitive, and it is often difficult for young designers to break into the field. In July 2006, an Emmy-nominated reality television series called *Project Runway*, which airs on Bravo, entered its third season. During the show, 15 up-and-coming designers compete for an opportunity to put on their own fashion show and have a greatly enhanced chance to break into the fashion world.

The show's host, Heidi Klum, is a supermodel who has appeared on the covers of virtually all major fashion magazines. Klum heads a panel of judges who eliminate one contestant each week until only three remain. Each week, the contestants compete in a challenge.

In the fourth week of the third season, the remaining 12 contestants were given 30 minutes in which to sketch a three-piece look for Macy's INC clothing line. The top four sketches were chosen, and the designers of those became team leaders to the remaining contestants. The four teams were given two days in which to create their look. The judges collaborated and selected a winner, but they did not reveal the winner of the competition until the following day. The winner, Angela Keslar, had designed a modern three-piece military-style outfit. The design was on display in Macy's department store window in New York City the day after the competition.

Two judges, designer Michael Kors and *Elle* magazine fashion director Nina Garcia, have returned each season as expert judges. Additional judges, including Vera Wang in the show's third season, appear on the show as guest judges. The judges offer their critique of what the contestants show each week. The final three contestants are judged at Bryant Park during New York's Fashion Week.

The first season's winner, Jay McCarroll, went on to star in his own reality special called *Project Jay*. The second season's winner, Chloe Dao, opened a successful clothing boutique called Lot 8. *Project Runway* offers its contestants exposure and recognition, which can help lead their careers on the path to success.

In addition to discovering new design talent, Wintour spends much time and energy on social issues, helping *Vogue* raise hundreds of thousands of dollars for global causes.

WORKING AT *VOGUE*

Wang was just 22 years old when she started at *Vogue*. One year later, she became one of the youngest people ever to take a position as an editor for the magazine. She assisted other editors, such as Polly Mellen. Wang came to highly respect Mellen for her ability to always look forward and see fashion for what it was to become—not what it had been. A friend and mentor, Mellen helped Wang learn the ropes of the industry and better understand fashion. Wang helped select accessories and locations of photo shoots, and *Vogue* quickly promoted her to senior editor.

Growing up surrounded by class and elegance, Wang developed a natural ability to spot quality workmanship and appreciate artistic detail. Working at *Vogue* now inundated her with avant-garde sophistication and offered her the opportunity to define and hone those natural talents. Wang later said in an interview on MSNBC.com:

> I think I always had an eye and *Vogue* made that eye even sharper. An eye is a new way of viewing something old. Everything's been done in fashion. It's how you bring newness to the concept. I mean, a white shirt is a white shirt, but how do you wear it? Those are the things that editors are always searching for, particularly in a picture because you only have so long to capture the magic of fashion.

During her work as a senior editor, Wang traveled the world and personally got to know designers, many of whom became her close friends. She learned much from these friendships with designers—the ins and outs of the fashion business, how to get things done on seemingly impossible schedules, and what is needed to make it in the competitive world of fashion. Numerous designers also took her under their wing to mentor her. Each saw Wang's potential and love of pure design. For a young woman with no formal fashion education, Wang had an exceptional informal education— taught by those who knew best.

In addition to working almost around the clock (she often worked well into the evening hours), Wang found time to hit her rebellious period during her years at *Vogue*. She managed to dance the night hours away at New York's Studio 54, a popular, chic disco and nightclub created by Steve Rubell, in midtown Manhattan. Studio 54 was known for being fast paced and wild. Drugs were common, and the mood was intense. Celebrities and noncelebrities alike danced and partied there. Wang would sometimes come straight from dancing to work. She went with a date or solo—at this point she was not interested in tying herself down to a steady relationship or marriage; she had too much work to do. She felt young and invincible and thought of herself as ageless. She saw no need to hurry down the aisle.

Wang doubted she would become editor in chief. After working as a senior editor for a time, she asked for a transfer to a position as the European editor for *American Vogue* in Paris. Her move to Paris was not a good fit for her, however. She preferred being in on the actual design—including being at the studio, the fittings, and the photo shoots. In Europe, Wang's job was grander, with the emphasis on public relations and wining and dining the high-end designers; there was none of the "dirt work" that she so enjoyed. Wang later said of the experience in Paris, "I'm not really a girl who likes to go out to lunch or cocktails or store openings. I felt very removed. It wasn't that I didn't like having lunch with Gianni Versace, it was just that

I wanted to be a designer still. Very much." The work in Paris clearly wasn't her style, and she requested to come home. Wang decided it was time to leave *Vogue* altogether.

Despite her dislike of the brief European portion of her time at *Vogue*, Wang's decision to take a position with the prestigious magazine accomplished what she had intended: She received a hands-on education in fashion. She had the opportunity to work with world-famous photographers such as Richard Avedon and Irving Penn. She enjoyed the work so much that she stayed with *Vogue* for 16 years (1971–1987) as a fashion editor and stylist. She spent her time meeting with designers, traveling the world, and selecting clothing for the magazine. The work allowed Wang to explore fashion and style in a new light. She later wrote:

> For nearly two decades as a *Vogue* editor, fashion was my life. I had the unique privilege of collaborating with some of the world's most creative individuals. From styling the fashion pages to working with designers, I was in a rare position to communicate with women. I also learned to hone my eye and trust my creative instincts to an extent even I could never have imagined. The incomparable training I received continues to guide my work today.

While Wang was working at *Vogue*, her brother Kenneth married Doreen Ma. The wedding took place in October 1983 at the Pound Ridge, New York, home of Cheng Ching and Florence Wang.

PERSONAL LIFE

After she left *Vogue* in 1987, Wang and her boyfriend, Arthur Paul Becker, planned a trip to Hawaii. The couple had met nearly a decade earlier at a tennis match in Forest Hills, Queens. At the

Vera Wang and Arthur Becker arrive at the Fresh Air Fund Salute to American Heroes in 2003.

time, Becker was working for Wang's father as a stockbroker at Bear, Stearns & Company in Manhattan.

When Becker first asked Wang out on a date, Wang agreed and the two met at a restaurant chosen by Wang. When Becker arrived at the restaurant for their date, he found not only Wang, but her entire family. Including her family in what she considered important was typical of Wang—she is very close to them. Although the presence of Wang's family intimidated Becker, the first date was the beginning of a lasting relationship.

In the years after that dinner, Wang and Becker dated on and off; both were busy with careers and not ready to commit to marriage or even a serious relationship. They did enjoy each other's company, however. In the time leading up to the couple's trip to Hawaii, Wang's friends and coworkers had been urging her to think about committing to a relationship and about marriage. Wang was coming to realize that she was not ageless, as she had once thought, and she did want to share her life with someone—so she looked forward to a relaxing vacation with Becker. She needed to get away from her fast-paced schedule and demanding career. She envisioned long dinners and walks along Hawaii's coastlines.

Her vacation did not turn out as expected. Instead of taking romantic walks and having deep conversations, Becker spent the days golfing, leaving Wang to fend for herself at the hotel. Becker knew all the hot spots for golf—he had previously lived in Hawaii and had a passion for the sport. It was not until the sixth day of the trip that he took Wang to a small town called Kukuihaele for an intimate dinner. Here, he asked Wang if she wanted to get married sometime in the future. She agreed—but the entire proposal lacked the romance that she expected. Becker did not propose more formally until two years later.

LIFE AFTER *VOGUE*

When Wang returned from her Hawaii trip, she spoke to her father about opening her own business. She had an idea of starting a shop that sold only tops. Her father was not interested. Wang then started to look at positions at existing companies. She received an offer from Geoffrey Beene, with whom she shared a passion for perfectionism and a love of clothes. Wang idolized Beene and was eager to begin working for him. He once said, "Respect for the body, respect for the fabric, respect for desires." Having been a premed student before turning to fashion, he had a great understanding of the human body and how to design clothes to fit its every move.

Despite Wang's and Beene's similarities, however, the job was not to be. On the day before she was supposed to begin her new position with Beene, Wang received a call from Ralph Lauren. Lauren offered her a salary four times higher than that offered by Beene. Wang felt that she couldn't refuse. She was eager to have a salary that allowed her to break free from accepting her father's financial support. Wang's sudden decision to not begin work with Beene cost her both his respect and his friendship: Geoffrey Beene never spoke to Vera Wang again. Wang later told an interviewer for *New York Magazine,* "It was very hard on me because I idolized Geoffrey. . . . But I had to have some money. I was 38 years old, and I was still living off my parents. But he didn't understand."

Wang worked for two years (1987–1989) as a design director at Ralph Lauren, overseeing 13 accessory lines. She also spent part of her time designing lingerie and sportswear. Wang was excited to design sportswear; she was a regular exerciser at a time when exercising was just becoming popular. She was able to create workout clothes to meet this increasingly popular activity.

During Wang's work with Lauren, she saw firsthand the difficulties a designer faces. It is not enough to be a great designer;

Ralph Lauren and Vera Wang attend a retirement party for Stan Herman, who departed his post as president of the Council of Fashion Designers of America in 2006.

you also have to be a great businessperson. The product must be designed, made, shipped, and sold—all within specific deadlines. If those deadlines are not met, the product will not make it to the customer and the designer makes no money. As in her time at *Vogue*, Wang was continuing her fashion education at Ralph Lauren. Wang's work with Ralph Lauren allowed her to fully grasp the practical "nuts and bolts" of what it takes to see a product through from design to customer.

MARRIAGE

In 1989, Becker made his formal—and this time romantic—proposal to Wang over dinner with close friends. He had arranged with the restaurant management for her engagement ring to be hidden in a piece of her favorite cake. She later wrote of the event, "Reaching over to hug him, I was genuinely filled with happiness and hope for what would be our future." The wedding day was set—for just a few days before her fortieth birthday.

Now the focus turned toward preparing for a wedding. With a bride as fashionable and stylish as Vera Wang, the wedding had to be spectacular. When looking for her wedding gown, however, she found nothing that fit her taste. All the gowns she saw were traditional. The dresses were frilly and gaudy and looked much like a decoration for the top of a wedding cake. Wang wanted a dress that represented who she was: modern and sophisticated.

The guest list for Becker and Wang's wedding started at 40 people but grew to 400. The guests joined the couple in the celebration of their marriage at the Pierre Hotel in New York on June 22, 1989. A 25-piece orchestra provided mood and atmosphere. The interfaith wedding (Becker is Jewish and Wang is Protestant) included both a rabbi, Charles J. Davidson, and a Baptist minister, Reverend Dr. Melvin A. Hawthorne.

In the end, Vera Wang designed her own wedding dress and hired a tailor to make it for her. The $10,000, 45-pound dress was a hand-beaded white duchesse satin gown. Wang chose a special fragrance for the day: She wore her mother's favorite perfume because she wanted to feel close to her.

Wang was disappointed in the bridesmaids' dresses (she had four bridesmaids), because her bridesmaids, like herself, were older and more sophisticated; the available dresses did not suit them. In one interview, Wang said her friends felt like the singing group the Supremes in their matching dresses. Nonetheless, Wang's older-than-average bridesmaids, who all had high-powered careers, got through the ceremony. Like many aspects of her life, Wang used this awareness as a learning experience and would later design modern, updated bridal gowns and bridesmaids' dresses for a wide range of ages and personalities.

For her reception, Wang wore a simple custom-made pink slip dress. In Chinese culture, it is customary for the bride to change clothes multiple times. Wang chose the color pink because it symbolizes happiness. Wang felt much more comfortable in the slip dress than she had in her wedding gown: The slip dress better matched her taste and preference for clean style. One of Wang's fondest memories from the reception was when her composer friend, Martin Charnin, sang an "impromptu rendition of his anthem, 'Tomorrow,' with lyrics written especially for [herself and Arthur]."

One aspect that saddened Wang when she looked back at the nearly perfect wedding day was that the ushers had forgotten to have the guests sign in. She later wrote, "[Arthur and I] were disappointed that the words we would have treasured were never recorded. While videos and photographs convey a sense of immediacy, handwritten notes are irreplaceable." Nonetheless, the wedding remained an event that Wang would treasure always.

4

Setting Out on Her Own

After their marriage, the newlyweds quickly turned their attention to beginning a family. Wang was unable to get pregnant, however, although she endured frequent trips to the hospital for blood tests and sonograms. Her overwhelming feelings were too much to cope with, and she quit her job at Ralph Lauren. It was a stressful and disappointing time in Wang's life. She had not anticipated being unable to conceive children, and the shock took a toll on both her psyche and her marriage. Becker was supportive and understanding during this sad time in both of their lives, however, and the couple looked into alternatives, including adoption.

During this emotional time, Wang's father proposed that now was the time for her to open her own business. Coping with deep despair over the news that she was unable to have children of her own, Wang wasn't even interested. Still, her father pushed her. He told her that, because she didn't particularly want a business, she wouldn't be as emotional and the business was therefore more likely to succeed. Cheng Ching was not merely trying to convince her to open a fashion business. He had a specific business in mind: the bridal business.

Years earlier, Wang had tried to persuade her father to help her start her own business, but he had refused. Now, with her being exhausted after the emotional strain of trying to have a child, he was offering his help. Was this the right time? Wang was determined to give it careful thought before making her decision.

Meanwhile, Calvin Klein, one of the world's leading designers, was trying to convince Wang to come work with him. He thought that Wang's contemplation about starting a bridal business was needless   he was certain that such a business would fail. He told Wang to contact him when she was over that idea.

VERA WANG BRIDAL HOUSE LTD.

Wang remained unsure of her father's insistence on bridal fashion, but then she remembered the void she had noticed in modern bridal dresses when looking for her own dress and those for her bridesmaids. She realized that bridalwear had not evolved over the years to the same extent that women had. Perhaps a bridal company would allow her the freedom to fill that void. With a growing sense that she could fill a real need in the market, Vera Wang decided that she *was* ready to go out on her own. Wang opened her own bridal design business on Madison Avenue in 1990. It was called Vera Wang Bridal House Ltd. and was located in New York City's Carlyle Hotel. The bridal house would remain Wang's flagship, or chief, salon. At the same time, she opened Vera Wang Made to Order salon, located across the street at the Mark Hotel. At the Made to Order salon, Wang would create dresses tailored to the client's individual measurements.

Wang felt scared when she signed her expensive lease in March, worrying how she would afford to pay rent if her bridal gowns did not take off. She was embarking on a risky venture, a business in which she had had no formal education. All of her fashion knowledge came from her early childhood exposure, her editing days at *Vogue,* and her time designing accessories for Ralph Lauren. In addition, it was a shaky time in the country's economy. Soon after Wang opened shop, the Persian Gulf War began and a recession hit the United States. The only financial backing Wang was able to find came from her father. Wang's father contributed $4 million to her business. She used $1 million of his contribution to redecorate the two-story Bridal House boutique to her liking with the help of architect Robert Rich.

Chet Hazzard, whom Wang had first met while working at *Vogue,* collaborated with her in her new endeavor, helping her get the business going. Before Hazzard worked with Wang, he had worked with Anne Klein and other well-known designers. Hazzard had followed Wang's career and admired her as a person. He was hesitant about the bridal business, however, because bridal wear was considered old-fashioned at the time. Still, Hazzard believed in Wang, and the two made a good pair. While Wang was busy with the redecoration of the design house, the company had no place to store the gowns it had to sell. Hazzard set up shop in a hotel suite in the Carlyle Hotel to meet with clients and complete sales until the redecoration was complete. For the first two years, obscure European designers designed most of the gowns sold. It wasn't until 1992, two years later, that Vera Wang would start to design wedding gowns.

During the redecoration process, times were hard and money was tight. Finally, six months after the lease was signed, in September 1990, the Bridal House officially opened its doors to the general public. *Vogue* ran a special six-page article on Vera Wang, which helped bring in clients during those early years.

For the first four years, few people paid much attention to Vera Wang, but she gradually earned a reputation for producing elegant and tasteful designs. Like her years spent at *Vogue,* the first four years in her bridal business allowed her an

Wang applauds her models after a showing of her wedding fashions at her showroom in New York City in 2001.

opportunity to learn and grow on the job. She had known nothing about bridal gowns when she opened her shop, but, by jumping into the business with both feet, she was able to give herself the training she needed. She researched the types of gowns that were on the market and was able to make changes in the industry based on her own tastes and preferences.

With her bridal designs, Wang showed the world that twenty-first–century brides could be modern, sophisticated, sexy, and sleek. She found luxurious fabrics and ensured high-quality detail and always sought the most perfect fit possible. When Wang designs a dress, she does not always pass it off to a tailor to put together; sometimes she picks up scissors herself and sews it by hand in order to decide what, if anything, needs to change.

Wang gave the frilly traditional wedding dress a modern lift with clean-cut sophistication and romantic elegance.

In addition to creating wedding gowns, Wang catered to a bride's many other related needs. This meant designing dresses for the bride's mother and friends, as well. She told one interviewer:

> As I was assembling a workroom, I worried about how I could keep my expert seamstresses busy and interested between bridal-gown orders. At the same time I realized there was more to bridal business than wedding dresses: there were usually plenty of parties the bride had to attend. She needed dresses. Her friends needed dresses. Her mother needed clothes.

CREATING QUALITY PRODUCT

Vera Wang and longtime business partner Chet Hazzard felt strongly about producing high-quality goods to present to their customers. Wang works with bridal fabrics that are not only white but also very delicate and expensive. When first looking for factories at which to manufacture Wang's designs, Wang and Hazzard did not find any existing factories that met their high standards.

Instead, Wang decided to have her own factories built. The fine fabrics would now have immaculate factories—one in Florida and one in Ohio—at which they could be made into gowns. In an interview, Hazzard said, "We're prudent people. . . . We didn't show [our clothing collections in runway fashion shows] for the first five years. We built our own factories instead. You can't work with expensive white fabrics around machines covered with oil. So we built our factories like pharmaceutical plants. Impeccable." Wang and Hazzard took great care in keeping their factories clean and running them efficiently to help ensure their high-quality products.

What began as a contained business (as proposed by Wang's father) was becoming an unexpected opportunity for her to unleash her creativity and intuitive sense of style.

QUALITY AND SERVICE

The bridal salon that Vera Wang opened in 1990 has become one of great prestige and respect. Walking past the outside of the shop, customers can see immediately that this contemporary store is not for casual browsing. A doorbell, rather than a freely swinging door, quietly signals that a person has to have an appointment in order to enter. Inside the serene space, gracious and knowledgeable consultants treat the 50 or so guests who come for their appointments each day to the utmost in exclusive service.

Wang credits her store's success to its continued extraordinary service. She ensures that her staff caters to all of a bride's needs, which reach far past the gown and accessories. When Wang meets with a new client, she asks, " 'How are you getting married?' rather than 'What's your fantasy?' Are you marrying in a church, a restaurant, a tent? Will there be 80 people? 500? What time of year? A dress must be tailored to the hows, wheres and whens. Then you try to marry the fantasy to the reality." Above all, Wang is looking to create designs that bring out the inner beauty in her clients. She said of her work, "If I can make a woman look tasteful and pretty, it adds to my own sense of self-worth."

The well-informed staff helps customers make decisions about flowers, jewelry, shoes, hair, cleaning and storage, and anything else about which brides or their bridal parties may have questions or concerns. Wang has insisted that "service is a prerequisite for anything relating to luxury." She added that consultants who offer fine food and drink at their salons help to make shopping "sensual and pleasurable."

DESIGNER FOR THE STARS

Wang never lost her love of figure skating, and, once she got into the world of fashion, she maintained close ties to the skating world. She designed costumes for Nancy Kerrigan for the 1992 and 1994 Winter Olympics. When Kerrigan's coach first approached Wang to design Kerrigan's costume in 1992, Wang refused. She knew that the task was going to be complex and difficult—skaters need an evening-gown look with the movement allowed by a swimsuit. The fabric needed careful consideration: It had to be stretchy and allow for a wide range of motion. In the end, however, Wang agreed. The 1992 costume Wang designed for Kerrigan made the cover of *Life's* Year in Pictures.

In 1994, Wang designed a simple, champagne-colored, hand-beaded skating dress that helped make her a worldwide name. Critics and fans alike thought that Kerrigan was the best-dressed skater in the 1994 Olympics. Wang continues to design skating costumes for Olympic figure skaters today. Michelle Kwan hired Wang frequently to design her numerous skating costumes each year.

As her bridal business got underway, Wang gradually included special occasion dresses, eveningwear, shoes, furs, fragrance, eyewear, handbags, china, and crystal. Moving from wedding gowns to special occasion dresses in 1993 and then to eveningwear in 1994 was not a stretch for Wang. She considers all of it similar—it is all costuming. Wang's costumes differed from those of many designers, however: The designs were minimalist, with classic lines and simple beauty. Wang believes that less is more. She rarely uses belts, which cut the bodyline in half. She doesn't like excessive ruffles or glitz, and she is always looking to simplify to find the perfect fit and look.

Wang has numerous celebrity friends, including two close friends, Holly Hunter and Sharon Stone. In 1993, Wang designed an old-fashioned blond satin ball gown for Stone, which

Actress Sharon Stone turns heads in a velvet Vera Wang dress at the sixteenth annual Council of Fashion Designers of America Awards at Lincoln Center.

Stone wore to the Academy Awards. Tom Julian, an internationally recognized trend authority, said of the Academy Awards:

> When it comes to glamour and style, the Red Carpet has been a singular point of fashion inspiration. It's the ultimate setting where all eyes focus on the talent and attire of Hollywood's elite. The looks are one-of-a-kind, the designer names are a global who's who of fashion, and the gems always dazzle. When the stars step onto the red carpet, they set the international standard for fashion and make style history.

Oscar clientele continued to seek out Vera Wang in years to come. In 1994, Marisa Tomei and Holly Hunter wore Wang gowns; in 1995, Holly Hunter and Sharon Stone wore Wang gowns; and in 1996, Alicia Silverstone and Mare Winningham wore Wang gowns. Each year celebrities look to Vera Wang in the hope of wearing a custom-made Wang gown to award events, movie openings, and gala events.

FROM WEDDING GOWNS TO BRIDESMAIDS' DRESSES

In 1995, Wang opened Maids on Madison, located across the street from her bridal salon. Wang designed a line of bridesmaids' dresses in muted, sophisticated colors, available both in cocktail and full lengths. She also sells two-piece bridesmaids' dresses for women who want more versatility in wearing their bridesmaids' dresses on occasions after the wedding. These dresses run from $200 to just under $1,000. Flower girl dresses are also available at Maids on Madison. As at Wang's flagship store, Maids on Madison requires an appointment and guests receive the utmost service and attention.

Wang recommends that bridesmaids "take cues from the bride." Today, Wang sees bridesmaids wearing matching or nonmatching dresses. She designs maids' dresses with this philosophy in mind so that customers can choose between similar yet different looks. On deciding whether to go matching or not, Wang has given this advice:

> For extremely large bridal parties, conformity of dress can be somewhat tedious. On the other hand, each attendant in a different gown can be a bit distracting. Establish some common ground, with slight variations for each attendant: dresses in the same fabric but in different shapes; dresses in different colors but in the same style; all attendants in the same dress but carrying different flowers; all bridesmaids in the same skirts but with different tops.

Wang's bridesmaids' dresses were well received, and customers flocked to the salon. Wang had stretched beyond the bride's gown to include her attendants' attire, and she was ready to continue with her expansion. Over the coming years, she added products that would enable her to satisfy more of a bride's many needs.

5

A Designer's Life

Vera Wang puts all her focus and attention on creating clothing out of sumptuous fabrics with a perfect fit. She spends hours shopping, purchasing, wearing, and living in clothes—because that is what she loves to do. She also spends this time with clothes in order to figure out what works in design and what does not. She studies clothes, reads about them, takes them apart, and puts them together. Wang has said of fashion, "I have studied fashion from every angle—historically and critically, cerebrally and emotionally."

Growing up with a passion and understanding for clothes led Wang to design clothes of her own. When she first started to see women out on the street wearing the designs she had created, she would have an emotional reaction: "When I saw someone in something I designed, I would literally go crazy and be jumping around. . . . I was like, 'This is what I was meant to do.' I was born for this. Pictures are fun and great, but this is product. I have always loved product. You've got to love product."

Vera Wang believes in a solid background of apprenticing before setting out on your own. The extent to which she studied and learned—long before she set out to launch her own company—helped her become the knowledgeable designer she is today. Wang hopes to inspire young people to achieve their goals and dreams. She gave the following advice to aspiring designers: "Don't be afraid to take time to learn. It's good to work for other people. I worked for others for 20 years. They paid me to learn."

Wang approaches fashion as an architect approaches designing a new building: She builds up from a strong foundation and considers setting, practicalities, and aesthetics. Wang's background in dance and figure skating has helped her think about how a person's body will move in her design. She strives to make her clothing comfortable and practical, while still refreshingly modern and sophisticated. She never wants a woman wearing one of her dresses to an evening event to feel as if she has put on a stiff or restrictive costume. She wants the woman to be able to feel and look natural, to act and move with grace. Although Wang says this goal can be a challenge, it is a challenge that she enjoys tackling.

A GROWING FAMILY

After failed attempts at pregnancy, including fertility treatments, Wang and Becker decided on adoption. They adopted two daughters, Cecilia (born in 1990 and adopted when Wang was 41 years old) and Josephine (born in 1993 and adopted when Wang was 44 years old). The girls are both Eurasian, or mixed European and Asian origin.

Wang loves being a mother and giving to her daughters what her own mother gave to her: an appreciation for beautiful things and an understanding of the need to find a creative outlet for personal expression. Wang does not feel that her children have the same degree of deferential respect for her that Wang

Designer Vera Wang poses with her daughters, Josephine and Cecilia Becker, in New York City in 2001.

does for her own parents. The level of respect Wang feels for her parents can be attributed to the Chinese customs that Wang was exposed to as a child. Wang realizes that her children are more Americanized than she was and thus accepts the differences in upbringings.

The family divides its time among three homes. The first is a sprawling 22-room apartment on Park Avenue in New York City. The richly decorated apartment is sophisticated but simple. The living room is decorated in yellow and gold. Everything is in its place, and the feeling is one of clean elegance. Visitors find tasteful, artistically placed antiques throughout the apartment. The second residence, a summer home, is located in Southampton, Long Island. The third, a converted barn, is located very close to one of Cheng Ching and Florence's homes, in Pound Ridge, New York. The barn is more than 200 years old. Recently, Wang bought a fourth house, this one in Shanghai, China. Her father plans to retire to Shanghai someday, and Wang looks forward to spending time with him there.

Wang believes that enjoying life with loved ones and choosing a fulfilling career are keys to a happy life. As a result, when she is not putting in her many work hours, she spends as much time as she can with her two daughters and her husband. Friends of Wang describe home-cooked meals and a high-quality family life. Wang prefers get-togethers with friends and neighbors to occur at their Park Avenue apartment, which is also the most practical option for keeping the family together.

The girls love to shop with their mother, and they share her appreciation of and interest in fashion. Wang delights in watching what Cecilia and Josephine find fashionable and is pleased that, like herself, the girls show a preference for modern, cutting-edge clothes. Wang hopes that, one day, at least one of her daughters will find that her appreciation of and interest in fashion has grown and will express the same passion for and knowledge about clothes that Wang has. She would like to pass on her business to one or both of them when she retires. For now, though, Wang is content watching Cecilia and Josephine finding their own ways to express themselves and find happiness.

Being Asian American
A BLENDING OF TWO CULTURES

Vera Wang's parents held high expectations for their children—particularly in their study habits and their overall success. These expectations were in part the result of long-standing expectations present in Chinese tradition. Although she grew up in the United States, Wang feels that same sense of expectation in relation to her daughters.

When Wang was growing up, she was unable to spend time in her parents' homeland because Communism had taken over China and her family did not feel welcome there. It was not until 2004 that Wang first visited her parents' birth country. That year, she traveled to China with her father to visit his hometown. Of the experience, Wang said, "He showed me tradition, the Ming empire, what another China was. . . . I saw modern China. I expected bicycles and Mao suits and what I saw was a pre-Tokyo China with a hunger for Western culture. It is a wonderfully exciting period. It's so fascinating." Now that Wang has bought a home in Shanghai, she is looking forward to sharing a part of her parents' past and her own culture and heritage with her children—a part that she missed as a child.

Vera Wang feels that growing up in the United States has helped her become the successful designer she is today: "America brought me freedom and gave me freedom as a woman. In America we think anything is possible. The Chinese feel they have to work to deserve it. America gives you ease and nonchalance, which is what I try to do in my clothes." Wang does believe in hard work—she would not have gotten where she is today without it—but America gave her opportunities that she would not have had in China.

A FAMILY ON THE GO

Just as Florence did with Wang, Wang wants to keep her children physically and mentally active. The family enjoys figure skating in Central Park during the winter months. Although outings like that sometimes turn into publicity shoots, Wang focuses on the experience itself rather than the glitz that the media around her occasionally try to generate. The entire family also enjoys tennis and golf. Wang and Becker belong to the Atlantic Golf Club in Bridgehampton. Becker has golfed there with Bill Clinton, with whom he and Wang are close friends. Wang's favorite part of golf is putting, which allows her to focus and strive to reach a tranquil state before guiding the ball toward the hole. Wang enjoys golfing nine holes with the whole family at the end of the day. Wang's father and brother also golf: They own a course in Pound Ridge, New York.

Today, Cecilia and Josephine attend the Chapin School, just as Vera did when she was young. She is happy that the girls are learning the Chinese language and is proud to see them embrace their heritage. Wang attends parent-teacher conferences and special school events, and she volunteers when she can. She sometimes races straight from a school function to her office to do a fitting for a celebrity. The ongoing struggle she faces to juggle her career and her family life is a challenge she accepts. Wang supports her daughters and wants to see them blossom and succeed in their lives. Her daughters have filled a void and created a bond and love more powerful than she could have imagined. Wang told one interviewer, "As a mother of two daughters, I have great respect for women. And I don't ever want to lose that."

AFTER HOURS

Vera Wang once said that, if she had not been a designer, she would have directed movies. She would have enjoyed sharing stories about people's lives—their hopes and dreams, successes and failures. Wang briefly considered an acting career, but it was short-lived because she realized that there would be few parts for an Asian American. Wang still enjoys watching movies and television. She especially likes the Biography Channel because she finds people's lives intriguing. What else does Wang like to do in her spare time? Well—of course—she likes to shop. She'll shop alone, with friends, or with her daughters.

One of Wang's closest friends is interior decorator Lisa Jackson. Jackson lives just a few doors down from Wang, and the two women love to shop and spend time together. They travel the world to find good boutiques in which to buy clothes and accessories. Wang has even been known to bring an assistant on her shopping sprees, simply to have someone to help carry her numerous purchases.

Some people may find it surprising that Vera Wang's closet is not all Wang labels (although you will find some there). Wang likes the fashions of Yohji Yamamoto, Jil Sander, Louis Vuitton, and Marni. Foremost, Vera Wang loves to be comfortable. Although some designers would frown on the practice, Wang wears plain black leggings nearly every day. She thinks of leggings as similar to jeans—a staple to slip on and forget about. She first bought her first pair of leggings from the Gap, but when they stopped making them, she turned to Danskin. The bottom half of her ensemble rarely changes, but Wang takes time in deciding what to pair with the leggings. She feels that the top is what people notice and remember.

Wang is frequently seen wearing black or earth tones; she noted in one interview that she is "not a pink-type of girl." Opting for neutral and dark color palettes, Wang keeps her personal clothing minimalist in design and mood. She likes to keep her appearance natural and simple. She wears very little or no makeup. Despite the simplicity of her dress, though, her style is always modern, clean, and sophisticated—like the clothes she designs.

HOLLYWOOD GLITTER

Top-name designers clamor to dress actors for the Academy Awards. They know that the exposure the stars give them could lead to increased name recognition. Wang said of the practice, "I didn't have to solicit in the beginning . . . but I do now, because when I dressed Sharon for the first time she went to the Oscars, it caused such a fashion stir. No one for years had taken the Oscars very seriously from a sartorial point of view. Now it is like a war."

Goldie Hawn, Meg Ryan, and Holly Hunter all wore Vera Wang creations in 1997. Meg Ryan's was a navy blue silk jersey evening dress. In 1998, Sharon Stone's attire received much attention. She wore her husband's white cotton dress shirt with a full-length lavender Vera Wang skirt. The wrap skirt was elegantly cinched in back and fastened with a dragonfly pin. The look went against Hollywood's traditional strapless ball gown but received rave reviews and recognition. Stone looked elegant and chic. Not long before the Academy Awards, Stone had worn a Wang wedding gown for her marriage to Phil Bronstein. Wang had designed a simple, elegant pink chiffon dress for her friend. Wang once said of Sharon Stone, "She has the looks, the devil-may-care attitude and the love of fashion." In 2000, Jane Fonda wore a fitted, modern gown to the Academy Awards with fingerless leather gloves, all designed by Vera Wang.

In addition to celebrities, Wang took on a project designing gowns for Mattel's Barbie doll. Other designers, including Givenchy, Versace, Dolce & Gabbana, and Gucci, also designed clothes for Barbie. Wang's "Vera Wang Barbie" became available to consumers in 1998. Wang dressed the limited-edition bridal doll in a contemporary ivory wedding gown with black velvet piping. Details included tiny pearl buttons going up the back of the bodice, a little black bow in the back along the velvet piping at the waist, and Wang's signature sheer illusion netting on Barbie's shoulders and sleeves.

Goldie Hawn (*left*) wearing a gown designed by Wang, presented the award for Best Original Song with Diane Keaton (*middle*) and Bette Midler (*right*) at the 1997 Academy Awards.

The following year, Wang designed an evening dress for Barbie in the Designers' Salute to Hollywood Collection. This time, she dressed the limited-edition doll in a lavender gown with an elaborate side train. The doll wore a long lavender stole lined in deep red. Accessories included a tiny evening bag that held an even smaller compact; a matching necklace, brooch, and earrings; and an overlay of tulle (sheer) fabric covering the side train.

THE NEXT STEP: LICENSING

Designing, manufacturing, and marketing bridal dresses is a business that Vera Wang had mastered. Although her growing business was making money, Wang did not have the surplus of funds needed to support designing and producing more lines. She *was* looking to expand her business, however, and to do this, she needed to enter the licensing industry. Licensing is the practice of one company granting permission to another company to manufacture its product for a specified payment.

Now that Wang's Bridal House was well received and successful, she could use that fame and recognition to widen the scope of her wares. She approached licensing thoughtfully and carefully, as she does all aspects of her business. She also depended on her business partner, Chet Hazzard, to meet with potential clients and help determine which products to move forward with and when.

Wang takes her time in deciding with whom she wants to sign agreements. She wants to make the best choices for her company and create high-quality products. Although she wants to ensure a growing and successful business, she does not want to sign away her name. She has become known for long negotiations when it comes to licensing.

6

Expansion Through Licenses

By 1995, Vera Wang was well known and successful. Her dresses (bridal and evening) retailed for about $10 million per year. Barneys New York, Neiman Marcus, and Saks Fifth Avenue all carried Wang bridal and eveningwear. As Wang's bridal store and evening gowns started to take off, she decided to take the next step in business—to begin signing licensing deals. The licensing deals with other companies would allow her to design products with her name on them, but the company with whom she signed the deal would handle production of the product. This arrangement would give Wang a steady, high cash flow to spend on designing new collections for her fashion business.

In addition to investigating broadening her wares, Wang also increased the number of her shops. Barneys' bridal departments in Chicago, Illinois, and in Beverly Hills, California now had Wang boutiques. In 1996, Wang launched another full-size bridal shop in Washington, D.C., located in the Watergate apartment and shopping complex. Now it was no longer necessary to travel to New York in order to buy a Vera Wang bridal or evening gown; people had the opportunity to shop Vera Wang throughout the country.

FIRST LICENSING DEAL

In 1997, Wang teamed up with an Italian shoe company called Rossimoda and signed her first licensing deal. Together, they developed a line of women's dress shoes. The shoes were produced overseas in a factory in Italy. They became very popular and were designed with Wang's bridal and evening gowns in mind. The shoes had a narrow platform heel, which helped make the person wearing them look taller and thinner. Some customers opted to dye their shoes to match the dresses they chose. Other shoes were available in satin, velvet, or suede.

Wang was pleased to see her company expanding, but she felt frustrated with the shoe deal because she was not able to be as involved as she would have liked. She would have preferred to see her shoes take on looks that were more unusual, and she wanted to experiment with the unexpected, such as unpredictable heel heights. Working with Rossimoda, she was not able to do so because there was a limited number of new shoes she could design each season; therefore she had less room to test out untraditional designs. Over the years, Wang was able to adjust the license, making her somewhat more at ease with the agreement.

Wang loves shoes and their ability to enhance the look of an outfit. She told an interviewer that some of her friends buy 20 pairs of shoes for every one jacket that they buy. Wang confessed to buying about 200 pairs of shoes on average each year. Her favorites include Gucci, Prada, Robert Clergerie, and Manolo Blahnik. That number does not include the shoes from her own line that she tries out to see how she can improve them.

Over the next few years, Wang continued to take on new licensing agreements: She signed deals with Coty for his and hers fragrances, with Waterford Wedgwood for china and crystal, and with Syratech for silver plates and glasses. Chet Hazzard worked closely with Wang to ensure that the timing of the licenses was appropriate for successful growth in the company.

EXPANSION

Vera Wang's first New York fashion show occurred in April 1998. Until this time, she and Hazzard had been holding off on doing fashion shows in order to ensure proper development and organization of their factories. The waiting paid off. Wang's eveningwear was a huge success on the runway. The blue, turquoise, and coral color palette of old Havana inspired her. Halter necks, low backs, and matte beads wowed reviewers. Store buyers were more than ready to stock their shelves with Wang creations.

Until then, Wang's original bridal- and eveningwear designs had been available at her flagship store and her wedding gowns were available at upscale department stores around the country. In 1998, Wang opened a full, 800-square-foot boutique that carried not only bridal and bridesmaids' dresses, but also eveningwear, shoes, and accessories in San Francisco's Saks Fifth Avenue. The additional boutique was a reflection of Wang's growing success and customer demand.

In 1999, Chet Hazzard met with Unilever Cosmetics International executive Laura Lee Miller to discuss possibilities for a Vera Wang fragrance. The fragrance would be intended for brides to wear on their wedding day. Unilever knew that consumers thought about classic style and taste when they thought about Vera Wang, so a fine perfume was a logical next product. It took a year of negotiations before Wang finally signed a licensing agreement with Unilever.

In another area, however, Wang was ready to take on her second licensing agreement. In 1999, she completed a deal with

Models wear evening gowns from Wang's Spring 1999 collection during her show in New York City's Bryant Park.

the Newmont Group for designs in leathers and furs. This license allowed Wang to design specialized accessory pieces for her bridal- and eveningwear. Although she did not expect this deal to bring in large amounts of money, Wang thought that the new pieces were necessary to accompany her high-end collections. A slim leather belt, a fur neckline, or a leather handbag would be just the right touch to complete a Vera Wang outfit.

When Wang presented her second fashion show in fall 1999 in Miami Beach, she turned it into a fund-raiser. Wang gave the money raised at the show to two AIDS organizations. Shortly afterward, the Council of Fashion Designers of America (CFDA), an association of America's top fashion and accessory designers, elected Wang to their board.

10-YEAR ANNIVERSARY

The year 2000 marked the 10-year anniversary of Wang's bridal business. The flagship salon on Madison Avenue had become one of the world's most respected bridal shops. Wang decided to expand and renovate her original New York store. She purchased the space adjacent to the original store; the new space would house her bridesmaid collection, footwear collections, and accessories.

Also in that year, Wang hired a stylist, Lori Goldstein. A stylist aids a designer in decisions, from concept to runway. Goldstein worked for renowned photographers Annie Leibowitz and Steven Meisel before joining Vera Wang's team. As designers' jobs have become more time consuming, they have come to rely on stylists to help track fashion trends and keep up with what other designers are preparing and presenting. With Wang's increased collections and accessories, she needs others' opinions and ideas to help create her final product.

After a year of negotiation, Wang signed an exclusive licensing agreement with Unilever Cosmetics International in March 2000. She could now begin to develop her first fragrance. One benefit to working with Unilever is that the company looks at not only short-term plans but also long-term plans for its products. Wang was envisioning taking her company's products global, so this was a solid business partnership.

Wang considered creating a fragrance to be an opportunity to reach customers who could not afford or were not planning to buy one of her dresses. She looked forward to capturing her ideas of romance in a fragrance for women. Over the next year, Vera Wang and her team developed a scent, working to find what she believed to represent intimacy between a man and woman.

2000 AND 2001 COLLECTIONS

In spring 2000, Wang showed numerous wedding gowns, as well as eveningwear and a few ready-to-wear dresses, at her New York runway show. The ready-to-wear dresses were very modern, all-white garments of varying lengths with geometric shapes in silver sewn along the waistline, the hem, or the neckline. They were not as well received as her other lines.

The wedding gowns and eveningwear, in contrast, were widely liked and displayed the sophistication and refined elegance that critics and fans had come to expect. She paired the wedding gowns with simple, long veils that trailed solemnly behind the models as they paraded down the runway.

Wang traveled to San Francisco in April to present her fall 2000 collection at the Asian Art Museum. The show included a dinner to benefit the museum's upcoming exhibit called The Golden Age of Chinese Archaeology: Celebrated Discoveries from the People's Republic of China. Wang showed a very modern, sporty collection that included jaunty knits, crocodile coats, and tailored jackets. The film *The Matrix* inspired Wang as she was designing the line. She did not show any wedding gowns at this show but rather exhibited many eveningwear dresses and gowns. At this time, Wang was slowly trying to break her way

A model wears a pink dress as she walks the runway at a showing of the Vera Wang Fall 2000 line in New York.

into the ready-to-wear market. She wanted to create clothes that women could wear to work or to a casual party.

The full house at the fashion event loved the new, nearly all-black line. Wang kept the clothes classic and elegant, with materials like tweed, cashmere, and chiffon. She was pleased with the event and was proud to present her show at the museum because Asian art had been such a huge part of her life while growing up and an ongoing influence in her work over the years.

Wang's spring 2001 collection was dramatic and breathtaking. The eveningwear was glamorous but simple. She opened her New York runway show with a stunning deep orange zip-front hooded caftan. She also showed all-white dresses with impeccably clean lines. Some of her dresses had a solid background color with splashes of color that looked as if they had been splattered on with the flick of a paintbrush. Classic, all-black, all-purple, and gold print dresses also lit the runway.

NEW DEALS

The year 2001 brought in sales estimates of more than 10,000 custom-made wedding dresses per year. That year, Wang also signed an eyewear licensing deal with Couteur Design Group and Kenmark Optical. She owned glasses by designers such as Armani, Oliver Peoples, and Mario Prada and was excited to develop her own line. Once she signed the agreement, Wang set to work designing eyewear that would complement her existing clothing lines. She looked forward to presenting a collection in 2002.

At about this time, Wang decided that a home collection would be a sound venture as the next step in broadening her product lines. She was looking forward to creating contemporary home products for her bridal customers' new homes. First, she wanted to give her upscale clientele choices of sophisticated, modern china and dishes. Later in 2001, Wang signed a licensing agreement with Waterford Wedgwood USA, under which she developed tableware, vases, wineglasses, and goblets. This partnership was Wedgwood's first license. Wang sold these products in her Madison Avenue boutique, as well as in department and specialty stores.

The addition of her latest licensing agreements brought Wang's name to even more people. Although she was taking on numerous endeavors, she and her team members put great thought and time into deciding what to add to the company. In this way, they were able to maintain high quality while adding depth to the company's name.

A CITY MOURNS

On the morning of September 11, 2001, catastrophic tragedy struck in the United States. Osama bin Laden had ordered members of the al Qaeda terrorist organization to attack the World Trade Center in New York City and the Pentagon outside Washington, D.C. The terrorists had hijacked four commercial U.S. airplanes. They crashed the first plane into the north tower of the World Trade Center and the second into the south tower. The third plane crashed into the Pentagon, and the fourth plane crashed in a Pennsylvania field after some of the passengers tried to stop the hijackers. The people aboard all four planes died instantly, and more than 3,000 people died as a result of the destruction that the airplanes caused. Businesses crumbled. People lost their jobs and their homes. Fires burned for 99 days after the attacks. The cost to clean up the disasters totaled $600 million. The events of 9/11 would affect the lives of the American people for years to come.

The day of the terrorist attacks, the opening of 7th on Sixth—the largest fashion runway show in New York City—was

SHOES, SHOES, SHOES

When Wang's licensing with Rossimoda expired, she signed a new agreement with Stuart Weitzman in late 2001; Wang designed the shoes and then Weitzman produced and distributed them. Each shoe included an imprint that read, "Handmade in Spain by Stuart Weitzman." Wang hoped that the change to a new manufacturer and distributor would allow her company to bring out more new shoes faster than it had with Rossimoda. The new shoe deal brought about shoes with unexpected texture combinations created to work with Wang's bridal and evening gowns. The shoes retailed from about $200 to more than $300.

scheduled to occur. Designers Ralph Lauren, Donna Karan, Calvin Klein, Michael Kors, Anna Sui, and Hugo Boss were to showcase their spring collections on that disastrous day. The president of 7th on Sixth canceled the entire show—which would have run throughout the week—and rescheduled the events for late October. Some designers withdrew altogether, and some opted for low-key presentations of their spring lines in their boutiques or department stores.

In typical years, 7th on Sixth is not a low-key event. It was originally created in 1993 in the hope of bringing American designers together in one spot to share their works and become known globally. Twice a year, 7th on Sixth presents fashion shows for designers' spring and fall collections at Bryant Park under large tents and in the plaza. For fall 2001, however, the prestigious event would not be. The tragedy of 9/11 stunned the world and caused people to stop and reflect on the fragility of life. New York City funneled all of its energy into rebuilding what once was. As the city of New York and the world grieved, so did the fashion industry.

Designers Giuseppe Zanotti and Vera Wang gather with a friend at the launch party for Zanotti's boutique in Paris.

A year and a half later, Wang was still dissatisfied with her shoe license. She switched to yet another agreement for shoes— her third in three years. This time, however, she did not sign a license agreement. Instead, she took on a partnership with Italian designer Giuseppe Zanotti. Like Weitzman, Zanotti manufactured and distributed the shoes that Wang designed. Customers know Zanotti for his use of lush fabrics from Paris and Italy and for doing part of the shoe production by hand. It was this level of detail and luxury that Wang and Hazzard wanted reflected in their shoes. As a result, the shoes sell for a higher price than Weitzman shoes, retailing for $250 to $450. The first of the Zanotti/Wang shoes premiered in spring 2004.

7

Published Author

In October 2001, HarperCollins released Vera Wang's book entitled *Vera Wang on Weddings.* Wang invested $4 million in the book: She wanted it to be perfect. She tried to work with two different writers before deciding that it would be best to write it herself. Wang found writing the book to be one of the most challenging projects she has undertaken, and she was pleased with the results. In an interview, she said of the experience:

> It's a remarkable exercise to sit and look at your own work over the years. . . . To me, the book is about more than just weddings or wedding dresses. It's a metaphor for women's lives, their creativity, their emotions. It's a dress rehearsal for life—a support system for women embarking on such an important part of their future. And most importantly, it's for all the women who embrace my esthetic, but can't afford a Vera Wang dress. If women can get

anything out of it—a little bit of me or a lot of me, that's what's important.

Wang's attention to detail and broad range of knowledge on fashion was apparent in the final product, which was a huge success. The hefty, nearly 300-page book was bound as a coffee table book that measured 10 inches by 13.5 inches. *Publisher's Weekly* called *Vera Wang on Weddings* "splendidly displayed." The review also stated that "the photos from her own and other weddings add to the luxurious, intimate feeling of the book." *Vera Wang on Weddings* covered all aspects of planning a wedding, from the proposal to the reception. Wang detailed her thoughts and ideas about music, how to select the right neckline, and the importance of keeping to a budget; she gave her advice on choosing a cake, when to register, and what fabric to wear during a certain time of day or season.

Collaborating with Wang on the book was friend and mentor Polly Mellen, who had worked with Wang at *Vogue*. Mellen was the creative director for the book. Anna Wintour, editor in chief of *Vogue*, wrote the book's foreword. Full-page photographs by Paolo Roversi and others highlighted some of the many celebrity gowns Vera Wang had designed over the years. Wang dedicated the book to her mother.

The experience of working on the book left Wang with the realization that her wedding gowns had a much greater impact on people's lives than she had thought. The gowns were creating a style and mood around which entire wedding events stemmed. As people sent her pictures from their weddings for possible inclusion in the book, Wang realized, "Not in my wildest dreams could I have anticipated the creativity my gowns would inspire and the impact of the clothes we so painstakingly create in our design studio." Similarly, Wang "was equally moved by the beauty, grace and elegance of these celebrations. Each wedding represented its own unique take on a timeless tradition."

WRITING ABOUT SKATING

In February 2002, Wang had the opportunity to try her hand at writing again. This time, however, Wang was writing on a smaller scale. She wrote articles for *Women's Wear Daily* (WWD) about the U.S. Olympics figure skating competition held in Salt

AD CAMPAIGNS

Advertising is key to the fashion industry. Creating a mood and displaying designs in a setting that reflects the designer's vision will help a buyer understand the clothes. Wang teamed up with former *Vogue* colleague Polly Mellen to put together a powerful international ad campaign shortly after her company's 10-year anniversary. Wang hired photographer Stacy Apikos-Boge to take pictures that would capture her vision. In addition, Wang selected models that she thought would best portray her gowns. Also on the set were hair and makeup stylists, a prop person, and six staff members to handle the lighting, camera operation, and film processing.

In all of her advertising and public relations events, Wang likes to keep things simple and focused to help define the spirit of her gowns. For this ad campaign, she chose a velvet background with soft, muted lighting to create a romantic, intimate atmosphere. Apikos-Boge later said of working with Wang, "I enjoyed having Vera there. . . . We were pretty much in agreement about how the dresses should be photographed." Apikos-Boge works with Polaroid, which she described in an interview: "The advantage and beauty of using Polaroid is its immediacy. . . . But I also can alter the color and experiment. It allows for accidents, which I believe in, in art. The manipulation comes from exposure time, lens, lighting. There's a real honesty with it." From the intense three-day shoot, Wang ended up with photos that she would later use in advertising campaigns, in annual reports, and with other promotional materials.

Lake City, Utah. In her series of articles, Wang focused primarily on describing the figure skaters' costumes, but she also gave her own take on how the various skaters performed.

Wang opened one article by writing, "Almost from the moment I arrived at the airport [in Salt Lake City], I could feel the pressure. It wasn't simply the huge media focus on Michelle Kwan and her two American challengers, Sasha Cohen and Sarah Hughes, but the very serious issue of judging such a subjective sport. Not unlike fashion, no?" Having been a competitive figure skater herself, Wang understood the emotional aspect to competing and being judged.

Wang went on to say that Sarah Hughes's costume was "prim, subtle, [and] dignified." Wang described Sasha Cohen's costume as a "simple tank dress in pale blue Lycra spandex and chiffon with 'blizzard' bleeding." No doubt Wang's favorite was her own creation for Michelle Kwan, of which she wrote, "Her dress was among the only dark ones, in this case a deep purple with multicolored crystal flowers embroidered with gold bullion threads."

When Wang wrote about the ice dancing competition the next day, she described how overly theatrical many of the costumes had become. This costuming diverted attention from what the audience wanted to see—the ice dancing. Wang wrote, "The desire to be viewed as avant-garde or intellectual has given way to a kind of chaos in which the intricacy and beauty of the sport has been obscured by scary makeup, messy hair and sometimes dangerous dresses that hinder movement and distract the eye." Wang would like to see ice dancers tone down their appearances in order to allow the grace and beauty of their technique to come across in their performances.

Wang enjoyed following figure skating, a sport she still cared for. She was happy to outfit Michelle Kwan, whom she admired as a skater. Wang had been tentative about designing skating

U.S. skater Michelle Kwan performs in a Vera Wang design during the ladies' short program at the Salt Lake City Winter Olympics in 2002.

costumes when coaches and skaters first started to approach her in the 1990s, but she rose to the challenge and has continued to create simple yet elegant costumes for elite skaters.

8

A Wang Empire

Vera Wang sells about 10,000 bridal gowns each year to brides around the world. Most of the gowns range in price from $6,000 to more than $12,000. To make her gowns accessible to more brides, Wang launched a new collection of bridal gowns that range in price from $1,650 to $2,990. In contrast, her custom-made gowns average around $25,000, and a single gown can take four tailors six months to create. Customers should allow another two months for fittings and alterations once the dress has been made. Wang often designs special garters to match these custom-made gowns. Of her couture bridal collection, Wang wrote, "Whether [the bride] is schoolmarm or siren, flower child or princess, socialite or career girl, or a bit of each rolled into one, the bride should choose a gown that reflects who she is above and before all else. A wedding gown must always embody the individual."

Vera Wang wedding gowns are available at her original bridal salon in the New York Carlyle Hotel, Saks Fifth Avenue,

Barneys, and Neiman Marcus. Many celebrities, including Victoria Beckham, Mariah Carey, Sarah Michelle Gellar, Helen Hunt, Jennifer Lopez, Jessica Simpson, Sharon Stone, Uma Thurman, and Vanessa Williams, have been married in Vera Wang dresses.

GETTING THE JOB DONE

Vera Wang is without a doubt a workaholic. Her workdays are filled with major and minor meetings and frequent client consultations. Wang is intense and driven. She takes every decision seriously and does not overlook any detail with her products. Her daughters occasionally join their mother at work in order to share dinner with her.

When Wang finally gets home, she uses the late night hours—often from 11:00 P.M. to 2:00 A.M.—to let her creativity flow and sketch, which she often does in bed. Of this work habit, Wang said, "My bedroom is my sanctuary. It's like a refuge, and it's where I do a fair amount of designing—at least conceptually, if not literally. I spread out on my side of the bed, and I may be looking at books to get ideas, or just thinking things through." She likes to sip apple martinis, but she drinks no caffeine. Because she is up so late, she often is asleep when her daughters leave for school in the morning, before 7:00 A.M.

Wang, like her father, is a good businessperson. She knows when to meet halfway and how to find balance, yet she is also a perfectionist and will not settle if it means compromising the product. She strives to listen to her staff and consider their needs when making decisions. Wang said of her business style:

> I try to share a tremendous amount with my staffers. I feel everything: the tribulations of business, the responsibility to people who depend on me to feed their families. Those things are always in my decision-making processes. Art and commerce are often conflicting concepts. You have to make compromises because the

most cutting-edge things are not necessarily what sells. You have to find a balance; it's a very difficult thing to do.

Wang is not shy or reserved. Although she is passionate about what she does and incredibly serious when it comes to fashion, she has a good sense of humor and enjoys joking with her colleagues, friends, and family. (She told an interviewer for *USA Weekend Magazine*, "I have a pillow in one of my houses that says, 'Don't elope!'") She is also quick to say what is on her mind and demands attention and respect when she speaks.

Wang is always open to change—in fact, she looks on change as an inevitable and exciting part of life. She enjoys traveling to Paris or Bologna to look for inspiration and ideas for her new lines. In her office, Wang surrounds herself with samples, fabric swatches, photographs, paintings, jewelry, and other sources of stimulation as she designs new collections and comes up with new looks and new ways to design clothes. Vera Wang identifies with designers like Comme des Garçons and Ann Demeulemeester. These designers, like Wang, use dark color palettes and unusual shapes in their designs.

The moments she spends absorbing inspiration from her travels and her surroundings feed and nurture Wang's artistry and vision. Most of her actual workweek, however, is spent in staff and client meetings, resolving issues and juggling schedules. She said, "My normal routine is pretty much putting out fires all day in my office."

Wang's husband is also a workaholic. After working for Wang's father when he and Vera first met, Becker became chairman of BNOX, a company that makes disposable binoculars. He currently is the CEO of an information technology services company called NaviSite.

FRAGRANCE

February 14, 2002, brought the unveiling of Wang's fragrance, called Vera Wang. The fragrance is a combination of Bulgarian rose, calla lily, mandarin flower, gardenia, white stephanotis, and sheer musk. The Valentine's Day opening was a smash success: Saks Fifth Avenue in New York broke a record for the highest sales of a new perfume. Customers paid $65 for a small spray dispenser or $300 for a one-ounce bottle.

In 2002, Vera Wang launched her signature fragrance, which she fashioned after classic French scents that evoke memories of her time in Paris.

Romance and passion are the two concepts that inspired Wang in developing the perfume. She wanted to capture the intensity and intimacy that surrounds two people's love for one another in her blended fragrance. Her success was apparent from the number of sales, as well as the 2003 FiFi Awards for Best Fragrance and Best Packaging. (The FiFi awards are given out by a nonprofit organization, the Fragrance Foundation, which is also an international fragrance industry.) In addition to the fragrance, customers could buy Vera Wang bath products, such as soap, powder, or after-bath cream. After the February United States premier, Wang unveiled her fragrance at Harrod's of London.

Wang later created a fragrance for men. This fragrance contains mandarin leaf, yuzu zest, nutmeg, leather, anise, sandalwood, and tobacco. In addition to the fragrance, she included grooming products for men in the collection. Wang's next fragrance, called Sheer Veil, was lighter than her original perfume. Sheer Veil consists of champagne roses, violets, white lilies, and lavender. The elegant yet playful and romantic fragrance was an instant success.

Most recently, Wang created a scent that her daughters, Cecilia and Josephine, inspired. It is called Vera Wang Princess and is aimed at women ages 18 to 24. The fragrance is a unique combination of lady apples, water lily, golden apricot, mandarin meringue, pink guava, Tahitian Tiaré flower, wild tuberose, and dark chocolate, among other scents. Unlike Wang's previous fragrances, this one was manufactured by Coty, Inc. Wang used actress Camilla Belle in the ad campaign and stylist Lori Goldstein.

EYEWEAR

Wang's first high-end eyewear line was available for viewing in March 2002 at Vision Expo East in New York City. Vision Expo East is a world-renowned trade show that introduces the latest in eyewear from around the country and the world. The exposure at Vision Expo East gave Wang's eyewear collections the attention they needed to sell well.

Wang had always been fascinated with eyewear and saw it as comparable to makeup: The choices people make with glasses can change their whole appearance. Glasses can also define a person; Wang once told an interviewer of her former *Vogue* colleague, "Look at Anna Wintour. Those oversize sunglasses she wears have become a part of her identity." Wang worked to ensure that her eyewear featured unique shapes and proportions and that it felt weightless on the consumer. Like clothes, eyewear was about self-expression. Wang said in an interview:

> I'm obsessed with details and how they relate to the wearer. I visualize women. I do this with all my products. A woman can be an athlete; she can be a classic, traditional individual; she can be vampish. Any or all these personality traits can be part of the same woman. That's what I want to accomplish with my eyewear. I want eyewear that can be worn in all aspects of her life. It's all about self expression."

Wang's eyewear line is made up of two collections: Vera Wang Luxe and the Vera Wang Collection. The collections consist of prescription and sunglass styles. Some of her most famous feature buffalo horn, and others feature jewels. The Luxe, a high-end collection, is manufactured overseas in Italy and Japan and is licensed by Kenmark Optical and the Couteur Design Group. Oliver Peoples's department store sales representatives distributed the lines to department stores such as Barneys, Neiman Marcus, and Bergdorf Goodman. The Vera Wang Luxe Collection sells for between $190 and $1,200; the Vera Wang Collection sells for between $150 and $250.

HOME COLLECTION AND READY-TO-WEAR

With the licensing agreement in place with Wedgwood, Wang had been working on designs for her home collection. Her china and crystal launched in late 2002. The elegant, sleek, modern pieces became highly successful. Within six months of hitting upscale department stores and boutiques, three patterns from Wang's home collection ranked in the top ten best-selling patterns at bridal registries.

The year 2002 also marked the launching of Vera Wang's first highly successful ready-to-wear line. Until now, the majority of Wang's eveningwear had been made to order; in other words, the customer would come to her shop, be measured, have fittings throughout the assembly process, and end up with a custom-made dress. The customer could not enter the shop and request a "size 8." Ready-to-wear clothing is made in multiples in standard clothing sizes. Although Wang had tried ready-to-wear in the two previous years, it had never taken off. This time, it did. Wang was able to obtain licenses this time, which provided available cash to help the line succeed. With the millions of dollars she made from her licensing deals, Wang could buy fabrics and supplies and hire staff to help her create the collection she was after. It did not take long for Bergdorf Goodman to place Vera Wang's ready-to-wear collection in a prominent, third-floor location near famous designers Balenciaga, Chloé, and Marni.

Wang's spring 2002 ready-to-wear collection featured fruit-inspired colors as well as classic black. The dresses were sophisticated and elegant, with a variety of lengths and necklines, including halter, cutout shoulders, and strapless.

For fall, Wang went with an all-black collection that won her much critical praise. Her designs included looks that spanned fashion history: high necks and corset-like bodices from Victorian times, ostrich feather decoration and bias-cut silk charmeuse from the 1930s, a fencing jacket and matching

"MAKING CLOTHES THAT ARE ABOUT ME"

Wang struggled for about two years to make the switch from bridal only to adding ready-to-wear, but she was persistent and continued to make her ready-to-wear collections until they caught on. She told an interviewer for *New York Magazine,* "I was a total fashion insider who became an outsider when I did bridal. I've had to crawl out of a hole, and it was a huge hole. But I've finally done it. I never got to be me. Finally, I'm making clothes that are about me."

Now, the growing success of her ready-to-wear collections is serving as a springboard for even more licensing. Susan Sokol, Wang's president of apparel, explained it this way: "What the ready-to-wear does is create more visibility for the brand. . . . And these are the opportunities that drive the licensing opportunities. It's a domino effect—you can't have one without the other."

Wang's ready-to-wear clothes are more sporty than her other lines while still being dressy. In contrast to designing clothes for socialites who might wear a dress only once, Wang prefers to think that she is designing these ready-to-wear clothes for women who will wear them many times. Today, Wang's ready-to-wear designs are sold at specialty stores worldwide, as well as at large upscale department stores like Barney's New York, Bergdorf Goodman, Nordstrom, and Saks Fifth Avenue. Anna Wintour said of Wang's collection, "Not since Donna Karan has there been such an open, clear personality behind a brand in women's ready-to-wear."

In the near future, Wang would like to design sportswear. An avid golfer, she does not think the clothing industry is meeting the needs of women athletes with sleek yet fashionable designs. Wang would like to fill that need and design a sportswear line herself. Perhaps as her licensing endeavors continue to expand and bring in more money, Wang will have the opportunity to make this new vision happen.

miniskirt from the 1960s, and dresses stopping at the knee from the 1980s.

JEWELRY

Wang teamed up with Rosy Blue, a company that accounts for 7 percent of the rough diamond trade, in 2003. The licensing partnership allowed Wang to design a diamond and fine jewelry collection. The jewelry line, including diamond engagement rings and gold and platinum wedding bands, catered to Wang's bridal consumers. Wang also designed art deco jewelry pieces to satisfy her nonbridal customers. Neiman Marcus and Saks Fifth Avenue are two of the upscale department stores to which Rosy Blue distributes Wang's designs. The retail prices for Wang's jewelry range from $300 up to $200,000. Wang also created a line for Zales that started at $1,500. This line included nonbridal rings, necklaces, earrings, and bracelets.

2003 AND 2004 COLLECTIONS

Wang continued to produce two collections per year in her ready-to-wear that were gaining popularity and praise with each new season. While Wang works on one of her new collections, she makes a point of not looking into what other designers are creating. She likes her designs to come purely from her own ideas and visions. On designing, Wang commented, "I look forward to creating something unique for all women."

For Wang's spring 2003 collection, she kept with simple neutrals—black, white, and taupe. She used chiffon, tulle, and silk to create elegant, modern dresses, trousers, skirts, and tops. Wang loves to use tulle in her designs. She wrote of the fabric, "Originally used for petticoats and underpinnings, tulle possesses a charm and beauty all its own. Tulle can be feminine, youthful and extremely versatile, whether it is draped as a simple overlay or gathered into a full-skirted ballerina gown." That season Wang did some tiers of understated

Wang, center, with daughters Cecilia and Josephine Becker, who inspired the fragrance *Vera Wang Princess*.

ruffles that gave the collection a younger, more hip feel than some of her past collections.

The fall 2003 collection showed a hint of Asian flair. The dresses were mostly all black or all pale gray. Keeping her love of luxurious fabrics, she used cashmere, goatskin, silk, and chiffon. The collection was minimalist, with the right touches of class—for example, a glimmer of beads, a small fur shrug, or a touch of lace.

Wang's spring 2004 collection was classy and elegant. She brought in a 1920s feel with some of her pieces, showing lady-like cocktail dresses in lots of black, white, and gray. She had a few solid, brilliantly colored dresses that looked ready for a walk down the red carpet.

Wang's fall 2004 collection was sensual and romantic. That season, she chose a color palette in muted tones of purple, green, taupe, brown, and black. She set waistbands low on the hips for her slim-cut skirts and trousers. She used a wide range of materials—cashmere, chiffon, wool, satin, and fur. Her models wore their hair long and soft for the runway show. Heavy, dark eyeliner, with little other makeup, created a dramatic, sexy look.

NEW TEAM MEMBERS AND NEW PRODUCTS

In 2004, Unilever executive Laura Lee Miller, who had helped start a Vera Wang fragrance, left Unilever and joined Wang's company. Miller became the head of Wang's licensing division, called VEW Ltd. She added dishes, stationery, and lingerie to Wang's list of products.

In August 2004, Susan Sokol joined the Vera Wang team as president of Wang's four apparel lines: bridal, bridesmaids, dresses, and ready-to-wear. Sokol's responsibilities include overseeing sales, production, merchandising, and marketing. She had previously worked for Calvin Klein and then Donna Karan.

As Wang's company continued to grow, so did her responsibilities. Not only was she responsible for the creative aspects of design, but she also spent her time handling public relations, licensing issues, and bridal questions. Wang told an interviewer, "It's hard to juggle being a businessperson with being a creative person. You have to organize yourself—PR needs me for PR, and the licensing division needs me for licensing, the bridal people need me for bridal. I prioritize by going to the next collection that's due. And as the collections get bigger, it gets more challenging."

Wang presented some of her new wares, which she had created in a licensing partnership with Syratech Corporation, at the Spring 2005 Tabletop Show in New York City. She showed flatware, napkin rings, placemats, and glassware in addition to her dinnerware. The stainless-steel flatware included the love knot icon on the handle. She introduced leather with her napkin rings and placemats. Rich colors like blue and green, as well as orange tones, created a bold, yet warm, color palette for Wang's dinnerware. Wang designed the glassware, including lacquer boxes, trays, vases, and bowls, in vibrant colors to complement the dinnerware.

Wang went forward with another venture, again with Syratech Corporation, to produce Vera Wang Silver and Gifts. Toward the end of 2004, she was ready to present her Baby Collection for spring 2005. For this collection, Wang designed a baby cup, feeding bowl and spoon, teething ring, heart rattle, music box, piggy bank, and picture frames. Wang used silverplate and sterling silver to create the products. When a customer buys one of these fanciful, endearing products, a salesperson will place it in a dove-white gift box and tie it with a lavender ribbon. The package is topped off with Vera Wang's triple heart baby motif.

9

A Global Push

In June 2005, Vera Wang won the title of Womenswear Designer of the Year from the Council of Fashion Designers of America (CFDA). When Wang heard that she was nominated for the award, she was ecstatic. She said of the nomination, "I've been going to the CFDA since when I was at *Vogue* for 17 years and then when I went with Ralph Lauren as part of his design team and then for the past 16 years on my own. So this nomination isn't just a dream come true; it's a lifelong dream come true."

The dream truly was coming true. Wang had spent her entire life surrounded by high fashion. She taught herself the ins and outs of the fashion industry by living fashion. Wang had once said about herself, "I do think I know more about clothes than any 500 designers, because there's nothing like wearing them. You buy them, you study them, and you start to understand how they're crafted. I was never a socialite who wore borrowed clothes to parties— I lived them!"

Wang accepts the Womenswear Designer of the Year Award at the Council of Fashion Designers of America's 2005 Fashion Awards in New York City.

Other nominees for the prestigious CFDA award were Marc Jacobs and Ralph Rucci. On accepting her award at the New York Public Library, Wang told the audience, "I'm really incredibly honored. Even at my age dreams in life can really come true."

Wang has appeared on numerous television shows. She has made guest appearances on shows such as *Style Star* and *Fashion in Focus*. Wang appeared on *The Oprah Winfrey Show* in 2003 for Winfrey's "Women in Power" episode. Along with Wang, Oprah Winfrey interviewed National Security Advisor Condoleezza Rice and eBay CEO Meg Whitman on the show. More recently, at the end of 2005, Wang appeared on *The Ellen DeGeneres Show*.

Behind the scenes, Wang has also designed shoes, wedding dresses, and evening gowns for television programs and movies. She designed the wedding dresses in the 1998 movie *The Parent Trap* and the 2000 movie *Four Dogs Playing Poker*. She designed the shoes that Sharon Stone wore in *The Muse* in 1999.

LOSSES

On January 17, 2004, Vera's beloved mother, Florence Wu Wang, died, surrounded by her immediate family. Florence had been a leading role model and advocate for the arts and fashion in Wang's life. She had been sick for many years before her death, and Wang and her family mourned the loss. Wang wrote of her mother, "I owe every wonderful thing in my life to her."

A year later, Wang endured another sad loss. Her longtime business partner, Chet Hazzard, died at the age of 50 of respiratory failure as a result of AIDS. His impact on Wang's company had been great, and his friendship, presence, guidance, and knowledge would be greatly missed by Wang. In her book, *Vera Wang on Weddings*, Wang wrote of Hazzard in the acknowledgments: "His business acumen, instincts and selflessness have been essential in helping me to realize my lifelong dream of becoming a designer."

The reflection of designer Vera Wang is framed in a mirror by the artwork of Henri Matisse, whose artwork inspired her 2005 collection.

2005 COLLECTIONS

Bergdorf Goodman hosted a summer 2005 trunk show in New York in which Vera Wang's clothes were well-received. She showed off not only her eveningwear, but also sportswear and casual clothes. Wang even signed a deal with Bergdorfs to sell her line exclusively at that store.

For her 2005 spring ready-to-wear collection, Wang went with inspiration she found while visiting the Metropolitan Museum of Art and looking at the Henri Matisse exhibit. This collection boasted artsy dresses with a feel of luxury and elegance. She used materials such as crepe de chine (a silk crepe used for dresses and blouses), georgette (a sheer, sensuous fabric), charmeuse (a shiny, luxurious fabric often used for undergarments), cashmere, and knits. Her neutral palette consisted of ivory, navy blue, brown, black, and taupe. Occasionally, she slipped in a touch of color or carefully placed sequins and beads.

When Vera Wang presented her fall 2005 ready-to-wear collection, the velvet separates and floating chiffon dresses received mixed reviews from critics. Wang's color palette consisted of greens, browns, and golds. Despite critics' uncertainty about some of her choices, like a fur bonnet tied under the chin, they praised other choices, such as full velvet jackets with pleats and the finely detailed elegance that had come to be expected from Wang. Wang said of her collection:

> [My inspiration] was Flemish painting, because they were painters that loved to explore light and illumination of color and the fact that colors could even be dark, but they could shine. So, this is very much a collection about mixing all different textures and all different tonalities. And I loved it, because it had a bit of the classic, but then we really twisted the shapes around and the combinations around a lot.

INTERNATIONAL FASHION DESIGNER OF THE YEAR

In January 2006, Vera Wang accepted the China Fashion Award (CFA) as International Fashion Designer of the Year in Shanghai, China. She traveled to China to receive the award. It was only her second visit to China. Wang said, "My take on Shanghai is modern, forward-thinking. I saw incredible steel-and-glass buildings going up . . ." She was happy to be there and was pleased to feel in touch with her culture. Receiving this award made her the first Chinese-American fashion designer to be globally recognized.

SEAMLESS

Douglas Keeve, a fashion photographer and filmmaker, created a feature-length documentary called *Seamless* in 2005. Ten years earlier, he had directed *Unzipped*, a documentary about high fashion that focused on designer Isaac Mizrahi. *Unzipped* won an Audience Award from the Sundance Film Festival.

Seamless spotlights three up-and-coming finalists in a fashion design competition put on by *Vogue* magazine and the Council of Fashion Designers of America. The movie allows viewers to look behind the scenes at the complexities of the fashion industry. The documentary follows 3 of the 10 finalists through the process of entering and designing for the competitions. The designers have three very different approaches to their work, and all have their own design styles and personalities.

Shy and quiet Doo-Ri Chung is featured first in the documentary. Chung works in a space below her parents' dry-cleaning store, creating fashions that her mother sews and her father ships. She was born in Korea but moved to the United States with her family when she was four years old. Since the film was produced, Chung has become a successful designer, known for her minimalist approach and for working with jersey.

The second contestant, Alexandre Plokhov, avoids giving Keeve a look at his submission because he does not care to talk about his works in progress. The Russian-born designer today has his own shop called Cloak, located in SoHo, New York City. At this menswear shop, Plokhov displays his collections—mostly shades of gray and black—using the "Cloak" label. His simple shop has only a large table in the center of the room and bookshelves filled with folded shirts and sweaters lining the walls.

The third finalist that Keeve followed is the duo of Lazaro Hernandez and Jack McCollough. The youngest entrants, this design pair met while attending school together at New York's Parsons School of Design. Barneys bought the collection that they created during their senior year there.

HALEKULANI HOTEL

In 2005, Wang undertook a new venture. She designed an exclusive suite at the Halekulani (which translates to "house befitting heaven") Hotel in Honolulu, Hawaii, in which guests can relax in pure luxury for $4,000 per night. Beautiful Vera Wang products fill the tastefully designed and appointed rooms. In addition to the elegant and contemporary Vera Wang products, the suite includes rare furnishings from Hawaii and Asia. Wang said of the project, "I wanted to create a space with some sense of the local culture."

Guests enjoy breathtaking views of Waikiki Beach and Diamond Head. They find exquisite bouquets of Wang's favorite tropical flowers throughout the suite. The dining room is stocked with Vera Wang Wedgwood china and glassware; guests may dine alone or with up to four other people. Guests can relax with a deep-soaking tub or 50-inch plasma television. They have private butler service and can request chauffeur service from the hotel to the airport, spa services, and exclusive sightseeing trips.

LINGERIE

Wang created Vera Wang Intimates in order to produce lingerie. In June 2005, she signed a lease that would take over the eighteenth floor in a building owned by GVA Williams, a real-estate firm. Wang got to work creating designs in both intimates (which include camisoles, long gowns, chemises, and pajamas) and body veils (which include camisoles, bikinis, thongs, and hipsters). The collections are available in silks and cottons. With the lingerie line in place, Wang can better meet the needs of her brides-to-be. The collections were presented in 2006.

TRAGEDY ON THE GULF COAST

Awards, new ventures, and upcoming collections took a backseat to a tragic event in Louisiana. On August 25, 2005,

Hurricane Katrina hit just north of Miami, Florida. Four days later, the eye of the hurricane hit Louisiana early in the morning. A few hours later, much of the levee system in New Orleans collapsed, causing Lake Pontchartrain and the Mississippi River to flood nearly the entire city. The hurricane damaged coastal regions of not only Louisiana, but also Mississippi and Alabama. More than 1,000 people died as a result of the hurricane. It caused about $200 billion in damage. More than one million people were displaced as a result of the hurricane. Thousands of these were bused to neighboring states.

People around the world joined to help the people of the Gulf Coast region after this devastating disaster. Supermodel Naomi Campbell, along with 7th on Sixth, producers of New York's Olympus Fashion Week, and the MAC AIDS Fund, put together Fashion for Relief, a fashion show and auction. The clothes worn at the fashion show were auctioned off with the proceeds going to AmeriCares to benefit the victims of Hurricane Katrina. Tommy Hilfiger, Marc Jacobs, Calvin Klein, Ralph Lauren, Mario Prada, Anna Sui, and Vera Wang were among the designers who participated in the event.

ADDITIONAL PROJECTS

Best Supporting Actress nominee Michelle Williams and Best Actress nominee Keira Knightley wore custom-made Vera Wang gowns to the 2006 Academy Awards. Knightley's gown was a deep plum-colored Bordeaux silk taffeta dress, which draped across one shoulder. The dress was close fitting through the bodice, hips, and thighs and then flared out in a grand bottom flounce. ABC viewers voted it best Oscar gown.

Knightley donated her gown to the relief agency Oxfam's auction, from which proceeds go to end poverty in East Africa. Wang placed the dress on exhibit at her bridal salon on Madison Avenue while it was being auctioned during the month of

April. The dress eventually sold for nearly $8,000 on eBay to a buyer in Chicago. The money raised from the dress can feed 500 African children for a month.

In another licensing deal, Wang teamed up with Serta Mattress company. After doing research that revealed that mattresses were often the first large purchase a married couple made, Wang thought that it would be a good fit for her product line. Laura Lee Miller described the licensing deal: "We are thrilled to be partnering with Serta. This partnership fits perfectly into our portfolio strategy and provides an avenue for Vera Wang's strong brand equity and authority as a designer to transition to the home." Wang designed eight mattresses that range in price from $1,000 to $1,500. The mattress collection was unveiled at the Las Vegas World Market in January 2006.

As with all of Wang's products, her mattress collection uses luxurious modern fabrics to contribute to the consumer's comfort and relaxation. One-limited edition mattress set is named Counting Sheep for the Cure. The pink mattresses will benefit the Susan G. Komen Breast Cancer Foundation. Another design, called Sweetheart, echoes aspects of one of Wang's best-selling bridal gowns. Yet another features a triple heart motif. In July, Wang unveiled her Luxe Collection by Serta.

SHOPS AROUND THE WORLD

Wang is now making a push to open shops around the world. She opened bridal boutiques in Brown Thomas in Dublin, Ireland; the Pudong Shangri-La Hotel in Shanghai and Singapore; the Ritz-Carlton Hotel in Jakarta, Indonesia; and the Shilla Hotel in Seoul, Korea.

Brown Thomas is an upscale lifestyle, or department, store located in Dublin, Ireland. Since opening, the bridal salon has been booked solid. The Vera Wang Salon consultants help clients find their dream wedding dresses, as well as select lingerie and find the right makeup.

In Shanghai, Wang opened a bridal boutique called the Perfect Wedding, located in the Pudong Shangri-La Hotel. The Link, a Singapore-based company, will run and operate the boutique. As at Wang's flagship salon, appointments are recommended for visitors to the small shop. Although the boutique is exceptionally small—it has one dressing room, about 20 wedding gowns, and a handful of evening gowns—it displays the same elegance that has come to be associated with Vera Wang's name.

Wang opened her first lifestyle boutique in the Halekulani resort in Hawaii, where her hotel suite is located. A lifestyle boutique is one that carries a wide array of products for the home, as well as clothing and lingerie. The boutique displays many of Wang's products, including china and crystal, fine jewelry, fine papers (which include stationery, invitations, and notecards), fragrance, ready-to-wear clothing, and evening-wear. In February 2006, the boutique presented Wang's first lingerie collection.

Wang also opened a boutique in Athens, Greece, on Kolon-aki Street in June 2006. Three months later, in September, the shop had an official opening event. The shop, with its hard-wood floors and brushed chrome accents, features bridal gowns and accessories. Wang embarked on this venture after noticing how many customers were traveling from Greece to New York to buy her gowns.

LATEST COLLECTIONS

Wang continues to create new, exciting collections that get people talking. Although she puts time and energy into her non-apparel products and enjoys creating them, her love will always be creating fresh looks for clothes. In one interview she said:

> I see myself as a true modernist. . . . Even when I do a traditional gown, I give it a modern twist. I go to the past

The stunning off-the-shoulder Vera Wang gown worn by British film star Keira Knightley at the 2006 Academy Awards was later auctioned off to aid Oxfam's relief work in Kenya, Somalia, Ethiopia, and Tanzania.

for research. I need to know what came before so I can break the rules. I work with structure, with techniques, but I go outside the box and give it my own spin. I adore the challenge of creating truly modern clothes—where a woman's personality and sense of style are realized. I want people to see the dress, but focus on the woman.

Vera Wang became the talked-about ready-to-wear designer with her spring 2006 collection. She drew on HBO's hit drama *Deadwood* for inspiration. Wang wanted to go primitive with the color palette of artist Henri Matisse. She described her collection as part Wild West and part nineteenth-century France. The collection included nightgown dresses, smock blouses, and jabots (ornamental cascades of ruffles down the front of a shirt, blouse, or dress). Her dresses were cut to hold volume without looking bulky. As a result, some audience members compared her work to designer Charles James, who was known for elegantly structured gowns.

The models that showed Wang's spring 2006 ready-to-wear collection wore their hair pulled loosely back into ponytails and low buns or long and straight. They wore very little makeup; what they did wear was light in color and application. The overall effect was soft and springlike.

Wang designed her fall 2006 collection based on inspiration she found from the glamorous mood set in the movie *The Talented Mr. Ripley*. She wanted the clothes to capture the feeling from 1950s Italy. She also looked to Mark Rothko's paintings for inspiration. Wang showed her collection in New York City's Bryant Park in February.

To get ready for the event, Wang worked closely with stylist Goldstein, who helped in some of the design decisions and in choosing models. When Goldstein first looked at Wang's collection, she advised Wang to take out a jacket and skirt with big buttons because they did not look modern. Wang agreed with Goldstein and had the pieces returned to be re-made with two buttons instead of six. Wang's designs were sexy, dark, and moody. She sometimes paired something sheer on the bottom (a sheer skirt) with something dark on top (a black halter top). In a few of her designs, Wang tried going for a more masculine look, which was unusual for her. Fans especially liked an iridescent rose chiffon gown layered over a dark-red slip.

Wang and Goldstein selected models with thin frames, long limbs, and sculpted fac es for the runway show. The models wore their hair pulled tightly back into low ponytails or buns. They wore minimal makeup—mostly eyeliner to accentuate the shape of their eyes. The overall look was fresh and clean and directed the emphasis to the clothes.

Wang's 2007 collections, first presented in June 2006 at her flagship store in New York City, were inspired by the world of dance, drawing on Wang's love of George Balanchine, the Bol-shoi Ballet, and Ballets Russes. Wang created a lower-priced Lavender Label with satin spaghetti-strapped day dresses and taffeta evening gowns. She also showed a higher-priced ready-to-wear Resort collection, with adjustable drawstring necklines on taffeta tops and gossamer print dresses.

10

What's Next for Vera Wang?

Wang's business produces $300 million per year in retail sales, including her bridal, eveningwear, ready-to-wear, and licensed products. Her name has become synonymous with wedding gowns. Those who see her work feel her passion for style. Paul Cavaco, the creative director of *Allure* who used to work with Wang at *Vogue*, said:

> Vera loves clothes. . . . Vera loves clothes beyond loving clothes; she loves everything that has to do with clothes. This is not a make-believe love here; it's the real thing. Anything that has happened to Vera is a fallout of this love. It's her only agenda. So she is going to present you clothes in an extremely loving manner: beautiful clothes in the most beautiful way possible.

Vera Wang is currently working on developing a line for a chain store. Other designers have done similar projects:

Martha Stewart created a line with Kmart and Isaac Mizrahi created a line for Target. Wang considers this type of partnership to be one direction in which fashion is heading. With few people able to buy a $1,000 shirt or skirt, the market for affordable—yet fashionable—clothing is hot.

DISCUSSIONS IN PROGRESS

Haim Dabah is the chairperson and CEO of Regatta/Pacific Alliance. He has been talking to Wang about the possibility of a deal between her and Kohl's department stores. The potential deal would allow Wang to design a low-price collection that would be sold at Kohl's stores. All of the clothes would be produced through Regatta/Pacific Alliance. Because of the high volume in sales at this national chain, such an agreement could be quite lucrative for Wang, potentially bringing her $100 million over a period of a few years.

Talks are also in the works with designer Liz Claiborne. Liz Claiborne sells apparel under the Liz Claiborne label as well as other brands such as Dana Buckman, Juicy Couture, and Sigrid Olsen. The company is looking to acquire more upscale lines and move into a higher-end product. In addition, Wang has spoken to St. John Knits, a West Coast maker of suits for women. Discussions are in the works about Wang taking over the design direction for the company. St. John is looking to update its image, and Vera Wang could do just that.

Jones Apparel Group is also talking to Vera Wang in the hope of engaging her to create a sportswear label. Jones Apparel Group itself is on the market, however, so that may affect whether or not Wang takes the deal. With so many negotiations on the table with so many different companies, Vera Wang has ample options to consider as she looks at how she wants to next evolve her growing empire. As she does with all her business transactions, Wang will take into consideration her own needs,

A model walks the runway at the Vera Wang Fall 2006 fashion show at the "Tent" during New York City's Fashion Week.

her company's needs, and the fashion industry's needs as she contemplates what direction to take.

LIFETIME ACHIEVEMENT

In May 2006, at 56 years old, Vera Wang received a lifetime achievement award as a result of her passion for clothes and artistry in creating them. *Vogue* editor-at-large André Leon Talley presented Wang with the award from the Savannah College of Art and Design in Georgia. Talley himself received the award in the year 2000, and in 2001, the award was renamed the André Leon Talley Lifetime Achievement Award. After Talley, renowned designers Oscar de la Renta, Karl Lagerfeld, Miuccia Prada, and Tom Ford were honored with the award.

Other Notable Individuals

TOP ASIAN DESIGNERS

Derek Lam

Derek Lam grew up in San Francisco, California. He graduated from New York's Parsons School of Design in 1990 and then immediately began to work for designer Michael Kors. Kors quickly became Lam's mentor and helped Lam understand the fashion industry and the ins and outs of designing. Four years later, Lam relocated to Hong Kong and began work at one of the largest direct retail brands in Asia. On returning to New York, he again worked for Kors, becoming the vice president of design for the KORS line.

In 2002, Lam founded the Derek Lam Company. He gained respect and praise soon after his opening and his 2003 runway presentation. Lam creates classic women's clothes that are refined but soft. He designed First Lady Laura Bush's clothing for the president's second-term inauguration ceremonies in 2005.

This up-and-coming Chinese-American designer plans to continue to develop his reputation for producing classically American designs. His work with Kors and in Hong Kong gave him a broad knowledge and global experience that is helping to fuel his success.

Thakoon Panichgul

Thakoon Panichgul was born in northern Thailand, but was raised in Omaha, Nebraska, from the time he was 11 years old. Growing up, he loved photography and fashion. Before pursuing those passions, Panichgul studied at Boston University, where he received a business degree. Panichgul then followed his heart by studying at Parsons School of Design.

Panichgul designs feminine clothing—romantic and modern at the same time. Like Wang, Panichgul first worked as a fashion editor (at prestigious fashion magazine *Harper's Bazaar*) before becoming a designer. His collections are well received by critics, and celebrities such as Sarah Jessica Parker and Demi Moore wear his designs.

Anna Sui

Anna Sui (pronounced "Swee"), who grew up in Michigan, always knew that she wanted to be a fashion designer. Growing up, she was on her school's "best dressed" list. Ready to pursue her dreams of becoming a designer, she enrolled in New York's Parsons School of Design at the young age of 16. In 1995, Sui opened the Anna Sui boutique in New York City, where she designs hip, chic clothing aimed at young people in their twenties. Because of her success and popular following, in 1998, she opened a second boutique in Los Angeles. That same year, Anna Sui Cosmetics and Fragrance opened in Tokyo and Osaka. The following year, in 1999, Anna Sui Cosmetics found their way to Saks Fifth Avenue, Nordstrom, and other specialty stores. Today, Chinese-American Anna Sui, known for her vibrant, exciting style, has 32 boutiques in 5 countries.

Vivienne Tam

Vivienne Tam was born in Canton, China, and raised in Hong Kong. Tam attended Hong Kong's Polytechnic's Fashion Design Department and then arrived in the United States in 1981. In 1983, she founded her company, East Wind Code, Ltd. She did not stage her first New York runway show until 1994; then, in 1997, she opened her flagship store in Soho, New York.

Like Vera Wang, Tam has published a book, called *China Chic*. In it she talked about her love of Chinese art and fashion. Tam's designs are all produced in Hong Kong or China. She uses Asian women in her advertising campaigns and works to pass along her knowledge and love of Chinese traditional culture.

Luly Yang

Luly Yang opened a bridal store in 2000 when, like Vera Wang, she was unable to find a wedding gown for her upcoming marriage to fit her

(continues)

(continued)

needs. Her boutique, called Luly Yang Couture, is located in downtown Seattle. She uses luxurious Asian and European silks and laces to create her bridal gowns, which start at $2,000. In an interview she said, "We specialize in individuality because our brides are all very unique. We want to make sure that it suits her accordingly." Yang currently sells bridal gowns, evening gowns, and wraps.

People have made comparisons between Luly Yang and Vera Wang because both are Asian-American bridal and eveningwear designers. Yang said, "It's a great compliment. I'm flattered because she's incredibly talented and she has built an amazing business in a short amount of time." Yang has plans to build on her own business, hoping to expand to include a line of accessories, shoes, and men's clothes.

The Savannah College of Art and Design attracts art and design students from around the world. The college aims to offer the best in art education and to prepare students for careers in their field of choice after college. Prior to the 2006 award show, the college hosted a Vera Wang exhibit that was open to the public. The gallery exhibit highlighted some of Wang's materials and images of her works throughout her career. The exhibit offered viewers an inside look at a designer's thought process.

A final ceremony took place at the Trustees Theater in Savannah. It not only honored Vera Wang, but also presented the college's annual fashion show of graduating students' work. When Paula Wallace, the president of Savannah College of Art and Design, was interviewed by the *Atlanta Journal-*

Up-and-coming designer Derek Lam poses with Vera Wang and a guest at the CFDA's new members cocktail party at Vera Wang's New York home in 2005.

Constitution, she said that Wang was a "fashion icon who is already a legend and has an auspicious future ahead of her."

INTERNET AND FASHION

The use of the Internet by consumers offers new opportunities to the fashion industry. Designers' collections are instantly available for online viewing, and photographs from runway shows are on the Internet hours after a show. With more consumers exposed to more designers, more people are buying luxury brand fragrances, accessories, and dishes online.

Vera Wang is happy with the hype that the Internet is creating for designer clothing and products. There is a drawback, however: People are used to seeing something online and expecting to be able to buy it immediately. The collections shown at runway shows are not produced and ready for the public until months after the show. Sometimes buyers are disappointed to learn that, although they may see a fashion on the Internet, it may not be possible to purchase it at that moment. This challenging situation is compounded even further because fashions and trends change so rapidly—which means that designers must work even faster to get their collections on the market as soon as possible before they miss a trend entirely.

Although more and more of Wang's products may be available to buy on the Internet in years to come, she knows that boutiques and department stores are going to remain. She continues to maintain her high standards of service in her own stores and takes great care in trying to meet the needs of her customers with sophistication and a personal style that will keep them coming back for future visits. One way to ensure this is her hands-on approach in talking to her clients. Wang said of her flagship store, "I have found my shop to be an incredible way to stay in touch with clients and experiment with new ideas. I always showcase a dozen or so dresses that no one else carries."

GROWING LEGACY

Vera Wang has a passion for art, design, fabric and texture, and the movement of the human body—and all of it comes together for her in designing. When she designs clothes, she not only considers the appearance and fashion statement that the design will make, she also places great importance on practicality: "I can't design anything without thinking of how a woman's body will look and move when she's wearing it. When I design a wedding dress with a bustle, it has to be one the bride can dance in. . . . I love the idea something is practical and still looks great."

Vera Wang acknowledges the applause on the runway after the launch of another successful collection.

Vera Wang is intense and business oriented; like her father, she keeps a close eye on the bottom line. Wang understands keenly what will sell and how to sell it. At this time, she has no plans to make her company public; she enjoys the control she is able to keep with it being a private company. She told one interviewer, "One of the advantages of being private is that I don't have to answer to a board. It also gives me the ability to experiment, which is important for any creative person. Being private has also given me the chance to elevate who we are as a brand. We haven't grown too quickly, and that's been a luxury."

Wang believes in creating fresh looks for women that bring out their sensuality and feminism. She likes simple, modern lines. Of her trade Wang said, "Clothes are my passion and my knowledge." She has clearly made a name for herself in the high fashion world. Now it seems certain that, in the near future, her name recognition will spread even further to the average consumer.

Wang's career has been forever changing and evolving into the powerhouse it is today. She creates stunning wedding gowns that mix the elegance of times past with the sleekness of modern life today. There was a time that she thought she would not move past bridal: "It is horrible to say, but I was stigmatized by being a bridal designer for a long time. I am amazed I have been able to move beyond it. I had really all but given up trying, but I did it because [designing ready-to-wear] was my lifelong dream."

Vera Wang has accomplished her dream. She is a successful, trendsetting, elite designer of multiple collections. She still grapples to find a balance between her work life and her home life, as most career moms do. She said of working mothers, "In the case of [business] women who are mothers, it's always a compromise. And it's never good enough. You just try to do your best." Some days are more stressful than others. At the end of each day, though, she has both a job and a family she dearly loves.

CHRONOLOGY

1930 Cheng Ching and Florence Wu marry in China.

1947 Communists take over China; Cheng Ching and Florence Wu immigrate to New York City.

1949 Vera Ellen Wang is born in New York City on June 27.

ca. 1954 Wang begins school at the Chapin School.

1956 Wang receives her first pair of figure skates and begins skating lessons.

1963 Diana Vreeland becomes editor in chief at *Vogue*.

1968 Wang places fifth in the U.S. Figure Skating Championships in the pairs event; she tries out for a spot on the Winter Olympic Games but does not make the team; she begins Sarah Lawrence College.

1970 Wang spends the summer working at Yves Saint Laurent.

1971 Wang graduates from Sarah Lawrence College with a B.A. in art history; she begins as sitting assistant with *Vogue*; Grace Mirabella becomes editor in chief at *Vogue*.

ca. 1978 Wang meets Arthur Becker at a tennis match in Forest Hills, New York.

1983 Wang's brother, Kenneth, marries Doreen Ma.

1987 Wang leaves *Vogue*; she takes a vacation with Arthur Becker, during which he proposes; Wang asks her father to help her start a business, but he declines; Wang accepts a job with Geoffrey Beene but quits the day before she is supposed to start to accept a job with Ralph Lauren.

1988 Anna Wintour becomes editor-in-chief at *Vogue*.

1989 Arthur Becker and Vera Wang marry at the Pierre Hotel in New York on June 22; Wang and Becker endure hardships trying to conceive a child, and Wang finds out that she cannot carry a child of her own.

1990 Wang opens her flagship salon, Vera Wang Bridal House Ltd., in New York City's Carlyle Hotel and her Vera Wang Made to Order salon, located across the street at the Mark Hotel; she teams up with Chet Hazzard to run her

TIMELINE

1968
Wang tries out for a spot on the Winter Olympic Games.

1970
Wang spends the summer working at Yves Saint Laurent.

1992
Wang begins to design her own line of wedding gowns

1993
Wang introduces special occasion dresses.

1940

1994

1940
Vera Ellen Wang is born in New York City on June 27.

1994
Wang begins to create eveningwear.

1989
Arthur Becker and Vera Wang marry at the Pierre Hotel in New York on June 22.

1990
Wang opens her flagship salon, Vera Wang Bridal House Ltd., in New York City's Carlyle Hotel and her Vera Wang Made to Order salon.

business; Cecilia, Wang and Becker's first adopted daughter, is born.

1992 Wang begins to design her own line of wedding gowns.

1993 Wang introduces special occasion dresses; Sharon Stone wears a Vera Wang gown to the Academy Awards; Josephine, Wang and Becker's second adopted daughter, is born.

1994 Nancy Kerrigan wears a Vera Wang skating outfit at the Winter Olympics; Wang begins to create eveningwear; Marisa Tomei and Holly

1995
Wang opens Maids on Madison to house her bridesmaids' dresses.

1997
Wang signs her first licensing deal with Rossimoda shoes.

2006
Wang accepts the China Fashion Award as International Fashion Designer of the Year; she signs a deal with Serta Mattress Company to design mattresses.

2000
Wang signs a license deal with Unilever Cosmetics International for first fragrance.

1995　　　　　　2006

1998
Vera Wang hosts her first fashion show.

2002
Wang signs a new shoe deal with Giuseppe Zanotti; her fragrance, "Vera Wang," hits stores; Wang produces first her highly successful ready-to-wear line.

1999
Wang is elected to Council of Fashion Designers of America's board.

2005
Wang wins the title of women's wear designer from Council of the Fashion Designers of America.

Hunter wear Vera Wang gowns to the Academy Awards.

1995 Wang opens Maids on Madison to house her bridesmaids' dresses; Holly Hunter and Sharon Stone wear Vera Wang gowns to the Academy Awards.

1996 Wang launches a full-size bridal shop in Washington, D.C.

1997 Wang signs her first licensing deal with Rossimoda shoes.

1998 Vera Wang hosts her first fashion show; she opens a new bridal boutique in San Francisco's Saks Fifth Avenue that carries bridal and bridesmaids' dresses, eveningwear, shoes, and accessories; the Vera Wang Barbie is available to consumers; Wang creates dresses for the movie *The Parent Trap.*

1999 Vera Wang's Barbie for the Designers' Salute to Hollywood Collection is available to consumers; Chet Hazzard meets with Unilever Cosmetics International to discuss a fragrance; Wang signs a license agreement with the Newmont Group for designs in leathers and furs; Wang is elected to the Council of Fashion Designers of America's board; Wang creates shoes for the movie *The Muse.*

2000 Wang's flagship salon has its 10-year anniversary; Wang expands and renovates the flagship salon; Wang hires stylist Lori Goldstein; Wang signs a license deal with Unilever Cosmetics International for her first fragrance; Wang creates wedding dresses for the movie *Four Dogs Playing Poker.*

2001 Wang signs a license deal with Couteur Design Group and Kenmark Optical for eyewear; Wang signs a license deal with Wedgwood Waterford USA for china and dishes; Wang's book, *Vera Wang on Weddings,* is published;

Wang signs a new shoe deal with Stuart Weitzman.

2002 Wang writes a series of articles that cover figure skating during the Salt Lake City Winter Olympic Games; she signs a new shoe deal with Giuseppe Zanotti; her fragrance, called Vera Wang, hits stores; Wang's eyewear and china and dish collections are available to customers; Wang produces her first highly successful ready-to-wear line.

2003 Wang's fragrance, Vera Wang, wins FiFi awards for Best Fragrance and Best Packaging; Wang signs a license deal with Rosy Blue for jewelry; Wang appears on *The Oprah Winfrey Show.*

2004 Wang's mother, Florence Wu Wang, dies; Laura Lee Miller joins Wang's team as the head of the licensing division; Susan Sokol joins Wang's team as president of Wang's four apparel lines.

2005 Wang's business partner, Chet Hazzard, dies of respiratory failure as a result of AIDS; Wang wins the title of women's wear designer from the Council of the Fashion Designers of America; she presents new tableware at the Spring 2005 Tabletop Show; she creates the Vera Wang Baby Collection; she appears on *The Ellen DeGeneres Show*; she designs an exclusive suite at the Halekulani Hotel in Honolulu, Hawaii; she launches her lingerie line.

2006 Wang accepts the China Fashion Award as International Fashion Designer of the Year; Wang signs a deal with Serta Mattress Company to design mattresses; she opens a boutique in Athens, Greece.

GLOSSARY

avant-garde—Active in the invention and application of new techniques in a given field, especially in the arts.

bias cut—A cut that runs diagonally across the grain of fabric.

bodice—The fitted part of a dress that extends from the waist to the shoulder.

charmeuse—A satin-finished silk fabric.

chiffon—A fabric of sheer silk or rayon.

crepe de chine—A silk crepe used for dresses and blouses.

duchesse satin—A lightweight, glossy satin-weave fabric, such as silk or rayon.

georgette—A sheer, strong silk or silklike clothing fabric with a dull, creped surface.

haute couture—Literally "high sewing"; trendsetting fashions.

illusion—Very fine netting.

jabot—Ornamental cascades of ruffles down the front of a shirt, blouse, or dress.

lacquer—A glossy, resinous material used as a surface coating.

licensing—Official or legal permission to do or own a specified thing.

piping—A narrow tube of fabric, sometimes enclosing a cord, used for trimming seams and edges, as of slipcovers.

ready-to-wear—Marketed in a finished condition in standard sizes.

stole—A woman's long scarf of cloth or fur worn about the shoulders.

trunk show—A collection of a designer's most recent work.

tulle—A fine, often starched net of silk, rayon, or nylon, used specially for veils, tutus, or gowns.

BIBLIOGRAPHY

BOOKS

Breward, Christopher. *Fashion*. New York: Oxford University
Press, 2003.

Jacobs, Laura (author), and Victor Skrebneski (photographer).
The Art of Haute Couture. New York: Abbeville Press, 1995.

McBride-Mellinger, Maria. *The Wedding Dress*. New York:
Random House, 1993.

Rawsthorn, Alice. *Yves Saint Laurent*. New York: Doubleday,
1996.

Wang, Vera. *Vera Wang on Weddings*. New York: HarperCollins,
2001.

Zilkha, Bettina. *Ultimate Style: The Best of the Best Dressed List*.
New York: Assouline, 2004.

WEB SITES

www.2020mag.com, "Feature Conversation With Vera Vision:
Vera Wang reflects on weddings, modernity and that most
incredible accessory—eyewear," by Gloria Nicola, Vol. No.
29:02 Issue: 2/11/02

http://abcnews.go.com/Entertainment/wireStory?id=1818803,
"Keira Knightley Donates Oscar Dress," April 7, 2006.

www.apparelsearch.com

http://www.asiams.net/Fashion/WangVera/vwang.html, "Risque
Business," c1999-2006.

www.geoffreybeene.com/beene_said.php

http://www.imaginginfo.com/publication/article.
jsp?pubId=3&id=1233, "A Vision of Vera," August 2002 Issue.

http://money.cnn.com/2006/03/02/news/newsmakers/
howiwork_fortune_032006/index.htm

http://www.msnbc.msn.com/id/9756475/site/newsweek/, "How
I got there: Vera Wang," October 24, 2005 issue

http://www.nytimes.com/2005/12/15/fashion/thursdaystyles/
15VERA.html?ex=1292302800&en=14c4aaa759982044&ei=

5088&partner=rssnyt&emc=rss, "Vera Wang's Business Is No Longer All Dressed in White," published December 15, 2005

www.oscar.com/style/women/index.html

www.semissourian.com/story/1144284.html

www.style.com

MAGAZINE ARTICLES

Ma, Fiona. "Bringing Style to the Bay," *AsianWeek,* Volume 21, No. 38 (May 18, 2000).

The Atlanta Journal-Constitution (www.ajc.com), "Crowning Achievement," by Marylin Johnson, http://www.ajc.com/news/content/living/fashion/stories/0611SLvera.html 6/11/06.

Factio Magazine, "Vera Wang: the Designer Who Changed Bridal Fashion." http://www.factio-magazine.com/specialfeatures/des_VeraWang.cfm.

Furniture Today, "Serta's Designer line," by David Perry, http://www.furnituretoday.com/article/CA6301824.html?display=News January 23, 2006.

International Figure Skating, "ITNY Honors Vera Wang," by Lois Elfman. http://www.icetheatrc.org/p_p_elfman.html January/February 2004.

International Herald Tribune, "Taking China: Vera Wang's long march," by Suzy Menkes. http://www.iht.com/articles/2005/11/07/style/fwang.php January 10, 2006.

Newsweek, "Vera Wang, Fashion designer." http://www.msnbc.msn.com/id/9756475/site/newsweek/ October 24, 2005

New York Magazine, "Vera Wang's Second Honeymoon," by Amy Larocca. http://newyorkmetro.com/nymetro/news/people/features/15541/ January 23, 2006.

The New York Times, "Reviews/Fashion; Dresses for Individualists," by Bernadine Morris, http://query.nytimes.com/gst/fullpage.html?res=9C0CE2D9113DF931A35753C1A966958260 October 2, 1990.

The Seattle Times, "A Gown to Remember," http://blog.nwsource.com/stylefile/archives/lulyyang_011906.html January 18, 2006.

The Seattle Times, "Designer Wang shifts seamlessly," by Samantha Critchell. http://seattletimes.nwsource.com/html/living/2002476597_verawang07.html September 7, 2005.

Town and Country, "Designer of Dreams," by Janet Carlson Freed. http://magazines.ivillage.com/townandcountry/style/feat/articles/0,,292424_414968,00.html February 1, 2002.

Travel and Leisure, "Wang's World," by Shane Mitchell. http://www.travelandleisure.com/articles/wangs-world October 2005.

USA Weekend Magazine, "Straight Talk: Vera Wang," by Jeffrey Zaslow, http://www.usaweekend.com/98_issues/980510/980510talk_wang.html May 8-10, 1997.

WWD, "Going for the Prize: A Glance at the 2005 Council of Fashion Designers of America Award Nominees and Honorees," http://www.highbeam.com/library/doc3.asp?DOCID=1G1:132919276&refid=holomed_1 May 31, 2005.

WWD, "The Transformation of Vera Wang," byline Marc Karimzadeh, http://www.highbeam.com/library/doc3.asp?DOCID=1G1:139041565&ctrlInfo=Round20%3AProd%3ADOC%3AResult&ao= November 16, 2005.

WWD, "Vera's Olympic Review," by Vera Wang, http://www.highbeam.com/library/doc3.asp?DOCID=1G1:83752667&ctrlInfo=Round20%3AProd%3ADOC%3AResult&ao= February 22, 2002.

WWD, "Vera's View," by Vera Wang, http://www.highbeam.com/library/doc3.asp?DOCID=1G1:83752599&ctrlInfo=Round20%3AProd%3ADOC%3AResult&ao= February 21, 2002.

TELEVISION

Lifetime Television for Women: Vera Wang: Gown Gal, Lifetime's intimate portrait. First aired on August 29, 2006.

FURTHER READING

BOOKS

Bolden, Tonya. *33 Things Every Girl Should Know: Stories, Songs, Poems, and Smart Talk by 33 Extraordinary Women.* New York: Crown Books for Young Readers, 1998.

Drudi, Elisabetta, *Figure Drawing for Fashion Design.* Amsterdam: Pepin Press, 2002.

Wang, Vera. *Vera Wang on Weddings.* New York: HarperCollins Publishers, 2001.

Watson, Linda. *100 Years of Style by Decade and Designer.* Philadelphia: Chelsea House Publishers, 2001.

WEB SITES

www.asianamericans.com. Exclusive information on Asian American fashion, food, culture, and more.

www.fashion.net. A directory of sites relating to fashion, art, and shopping.

www.fashion-planet.com. A monthly online magazine that covers everything fashion.

www.style.com/vogue/. Click on "Fashion Shows" to view Vera Wang's past runway shows.

www.verawang.com. Vera Wang's official Web site.

PHOTO CREDITS

INDEX

ABOUT
THE AUTHOR

ANNE M. TODD received a bachelor of arts degree in English and American Indian studies from the University of Minnesota. She has written a number of children's books, including biographies about American Indians and informative books about American history. Todd is also the author of *Hamid Karzai*, in Chelsea House's MAJOR WORLD LEADERS series, and *Mohandas Gandhi*, in Chelsea House's SPIRITUAL LEADERS AND THINKERS series. She lives in Prior Lake, Minnesota.